THE REVELATION LETTERS

PREPARING YOUTH GROUPS FOR CHRIST'S RETURN

D1532766

A Creative Study of Revelation 1-4

THE REVELATION LETTERS

PREPARING YOUTH GROUPS FOR CHRIST'S RETURN

DAVID OLSHINE

EMPOWERED® Youth Products
Standard Publishing
Cincinnati, Ohio

CONTENTS

Edited by Dale Reeves and Leslie Durden
Cover and inside design by Dina Sorn

Copyright © 2001 by Standard Publishing
All rights reserved
Empowered® Youth Products is a trademark of Standard Publishing
Printed in the United States of America

Standard Publishing, Cincinnati, Ohio
A Division of Standex International Corporation

08 07 06 05

5 4 3

ISBN: 0-7847-1197-6

HOW TO USE THIS BOOK

Acknowledgments

- A huge thanks to my administrative assistant Pat Bradley. Where in the world would I be without your eyes and ears and typing skills?
- To Dr. Terry Hulbert, a master teacher of the Bible and professor at Columbia International University, for your insights into the book of Revelation.
- To Justin Knight, youth pastor at my home church, for allowing me to try this material out on his students.
- To my soul brothers, Larry Wagner and Hule Goddard. My life would not be the same without you guys.
- And most importantly, to Rhonda, Rachel and Andrew, the greatest wife, daughter and son a guy could have. I am blessed beyond anyone's wildest dreams.

Talking about the future gets people's hearts pounding. The 21st-century has brought about a great amount of excitement, fear and concern. Because we have entered a new millennium, a lot of individuals want to know, "Are we living in the end times? Is this the finale?" Many people have turned to prophecy and the book of Revelation for hope and insight. People are worried about the future. Books on the end times are selling at a record pace.

What does God want to say to youth groups about living in the end times? Are we to panic? Worry? Or is it just simply a matter of "trusting God" and hoping everything will work out?

The first four chapters of Revelation give some practical advice on how to live, collectively as youth groups and individually as Christians. Revelation is more than a newspaper for the future—it is a manual for today!

Revelation 1-4 is about eyesight. John, the writer, sees visions of the resurrected Jesus and gives messages to seven churches. Revelation means to "unveil and disclose"; therefore, it takes eyes to understand its meanings. Each session in this book is divided into four sections: **Eye-Popping Openers, Looking Deeper, Laser Surgery** and **Getting Focused.** These lessons on Revelation are designed for small group Bible studies, Sunday school or youth group meetings. Each lesson is designed for about 35-45 minutes (so if you have an hour to meet, have a gathering time to eat lots of sugar!).

Eye-Popping Openers should get your students warmed up by providing relevant crowdbreakers, object lessons, stories or discussion starters that will get them thinking, talking and opening up to the lesson. This is a "hook" to get the "sand out of their eyes." There will usually be several choices, so use those which are appropriate for your group.

Looking Deeper consists of a brief Scripture commentary for the teacher. Use as much or as little as needed to "whet" your students appetite. Resist "torturing" them with too much information.

Laser Surgery features activities designed to allow students to interact with the Scripture text, including reproducible student sheets, creative object talks and more. Vary your presentation of the material from week to week, using a student sheet one week, a media moment the next and a spirited discussion the next. In other words, "Never do anything always." Keep your students guessing. Also included is a sidebar entitled, **"Extra Options . . ."** in case you need more!

Getting Focused offers some activities to challenge students' application of the main point of the lesson. Experiential learning is the key to this section. These activities should put "feet" to their faith.

Since the media (especially music and film) make up a large part of students' identity and often shape their culture, we have included numerous **Media Moments.** These sidebars include music or movie clip suggestions that reinforce the teaching of the day. WARNING! Preview all film clips before using them. They are not always obviously "spiritual" or self-explanatory. Weave these illustrations into your presentation of the material. Without proper explanation before or after, they might become simply entertainment and not a powerful teaching tool. Also, there could possibly be offensive material before or after the suggested clip, so know when to start and stop it. These choices have been selected with a perspective of "bridging the gap" with unchurched teens and "seekers" with little or no church background. NOTE: The start points noted are from the opening studio logo of the movie, not the beginning of your tape. Reset the counter to 0:00:00 when the studio logo appears.

PREPARING TO TEACH

Be sensitive to the learning styles of your teens. Some students are auditory learners, meaning they learn best by what they hear. Others are discussion-oriented learners and thrive on ideas and opinions. Still others are dynamic learners—preferring to actively "experience" the lesson by doing. Hopefully you know your students better than anyone, so be aware of their different needs and developmental issues. Mix it up; keep it happening. Use variety. Movement is the key. Each session is designed to be interactive.

Today's students like to talk . . . let them, even if their thoughts are bizarre. Ask good questions . . . questions that don't lead to "yes or no" answers. And, remember that the relationship you have with your students is far more important than the lesson. This study is only a means to an end. The ultimate objective is to lead your students to encounter the Lord Jesus Christ. The book of Revelation is more about the unveiling of the person and character of Jesus Christ than it is about prophecy or end-times events.

My contributors and I have field-tested this material for you. We have enclosed music, media resources, video clips and crowdbreaker options for a reason—to draw in the students, to create interest, curiosity and at times confusion. Don't feel that every session has to have a nice, clean ending. It's okay to let the students leave with more questions than answers.

As you prepare to teach, be flexible, discerning and prayerful. Adapt and change when necessary. Never let the students know what is coming next. Watch God work wonders as you employ effective strategies that win students over to his Word. And, by the way, have a blast as you teach!

Groups with access to media will want to plan ahead to secure videos and order CDs. The United States Copyright Act treats displays or performance of multimedia presentations, films and videotapes by nonprofit organizations (including churches) to a small group of individuals as "public performances" even if no admission fee is charged. The fact that the church or one of its members may have purchased the copy of the film or videotape makes no difference. To avoid running afoul of the "public performance" prohibition in the Copyright Act, you must in each instance secure the copyright owner's permission or alternatively obtain an "umbrella license" from the Motion Picture Licensing Corporation. To learn more about the umbrella license, contact the MPLC at 1-800-462-8855 or visit them on the web at www.mplc.com. You may also want to visit http://fairuse.stanford.edu/ for additional information on the Copyright Act and the "Fair Use Doctrine."

INTRODUCTION TO REVELATION

WHO WROTE THE BOOK?

The apostle John on the island of Patmos wrote the book of Revelation. John was the disciple of Jesus who also wrote the Gospel of John, 1, 2, 3 John and of course, Revelation. Four times the author identifies himself as John (1:1, 4, 9; 22:8). This is the same John who is referred to as "the beloved disciple" of Jesus. John was the only disciple to die at an old age; all the rest were martyred for their faith.

WHEN WAS IT WRITTEN?

The book was written during a time of intense persecution, probably during the time of Emperor Domitian, somewhere between A.D. 90-95. John was being "silenced" by the emperor because of his strong Christian faith and was exiled to the island of Patmos.

WHY WAS IT WRITTEN?

During John's time on Patmos, he received a vision from Jesus. Many of God's people had visions: Daniel, Ezekiel, Jeremiah, Peter and Paul, to name a few. These visions came to John through an angel. We will focus on Jesus' words to the seven churches. These were seven literal, historical churches in John's day. Some Bible scholars have suggested that each of the seven churches represents a specific time of history (or dispensation), but this is pushing the text a bit. These affirmations and warnings from Jesus to the seven churches do have incredible impact on any church or youth ministry today. Thus, in this study we are taking some liberties at addressing youth groups specifically, even though the original intent was not aimed at 21st-century churches. The Bible as God's Word penetrates all cultures and all times and seasons.

The book of Revelation is a thrilling adventure. We will cover only the first four chapters. Many of these words are from Jesus to seven congregations with recommendations on how to live out their faith. Some churches are outstanding in their ability to handle suffering, whereas other congregations are affirmed for their evangelistic zeal. Only two of the seven churches are without corrections from the Messiah Jesus. Each of the seven congregations is called to listen to the Spirit of God. "Are your ears awake? Listen" (THE MESSAGE). These messages from Jesus are intended to help the church get ready for his return. Each of these churches presents huge challenges for our teenagers today. Let's jump on for a wild ride.

DID I GET ANY MAIL?

John received a message from God about the person of Jesus, a revelation or unveiling of Christ. Many want to turn Revelation into a book about the future, but it is primarily about the person, power and majesty of Jesus Christ. This might disappoint your students, but Revelation is about seeing Jesus! That is why the book is called "The Revelation of Jesus Christ." It is not a revelation of prophecies or a revelation of the antichrist—it is a revelation of the Lord Jesus. If this book does not produce adoration and worship of Jesus, then we have missed the grand purpose of this book!

EYE-POPPING OPENERS

1. AGREE OR DISAGREE?

Ahead of time you may want to copy the reproducible student sheet on page 15 onto an overhead transparency.

To begin this activity, tell students, **"I need several of you to volunteer for a lively debate. Any daring souls?"** After you have recruited your participants, explain that each person has 30 seconds to debate each of six statements, which you will reveal one by one. For each statement, assign two small groups of students to represent each particular position. (One group will agree and the other must disagree.) Take turns letting a student from each group defend its view. Then, change positions on each succeeding statement. Be sure to reveal only one of the statements on the transparency at a time. Keep the other statements covered with a piece of paper until you are ready for each of them.

The debates on each of the six statements on the reproducible sheet will solicit many different responses, so be prepared to field them and listen intently. The statements are "hooks" to get the students into the topic of the day.

Allow a few minutes of debate and then conclude by saying, **"For the next several weeks, we are going to take a look at the book of Revelation. Let's begin by asking three questions:"**

- **When you think of the book of Revelation, what words or emotions come to your mind?** *(Some possible answers include fear, excitement, intrigue, confusion, difficult to understand, irrelevant.)*
- **Why should we study Revelation?**

LESSON TEXT
Revelation 1:1-20

LESSON FOCUS
Revelation is the unveiling of Jesus Christ and the revealing of things to come.

LESSON GOALS
As a result of participating in this lesson, students will:
- Discover why Revelation was written and to whom.
- Discuss the seven churches in Revelation.
- Make some observations about their youth group.
- Gain insight into the awesome description of Jesus in Heaven.

Materials needed:
Reproducible student sheet on page 15 of this book; overhead projector; transparency; blank paper

Show a clip from the video *Jesus 2000*, in which Jeremy Sisto plays the role of Jesus. The video consists of two tapes. Ask students: **"What do you think Jesus looked like on earth?"** After their responses, begin tape two at 42:07 and stop at 44:36. This clip shows Jesus spending time with his disciples at the last supper before his crucifixion. Did the video capture what students think Jesus looked like? Is the "Hollywood" portrayal of Jesus accurate?

Show a second clip that depicts Jesus after his resurrection, interacting with Mary Magdalene and his disciples. Begin tape two at 1:20:03 and end at 1:24:56. Ask your students what they think of Jesus' appearance before and after the resurrection. This session gives a description of Jesus that can't be painted or put on screen!

Materials needed:
A variety of pieces of mail; photographs; postcards or pictures from magazines

Moment

A great way to open this study would be by showing a clip from the movie *You've Got Mail*. (Use to explain the mailman concept—Jesus' words to John the recipient, who is to deliver the mail to churches located in what is now Turkey. These churches are approximately 30-50 miles apart from each other.)

Show the scene toward the end of the movie in which Tom Hanks visits Meg Ryan at her apartment and brings her daisies. Start at 1:38:28 and end at 1:43:25. He dialogues with Meg about this man she likes (he is referring to himself but she doesn't know it yet). She tells Hanks that she likes the same person via the Internet, although she has never met him. Hanks mentions the words "You've got mail."

(Possible answers include "to learn more about Jesus," or "to be ready for the end of the world.")
- **What does the word "revelation" mean?**
(An unveiling, uncovering, disclosure.)

2. SHOW AND TELL

Bring in a bunch of mail including some junk mail, credit card invitations, coupons and personal letters. Dump them on a table or on the floor in your meeting room. Allow students several minutes to look through them. Ask them to decide which pieces of mail are the most important and which are nonessential.

Then comment, **"What would you do if Jesus himself sent you a piece of mail? That's exactly what he did in the first few chapters of the book of Revelation. Over the next several weeks we are going to look at some important mail, personal letters that were addressed to seven churches in Asia."**

Ask students to think about this question, but not necessarily respond verbally:

- **If Jesus were to write a letter today to our youth group, what strengths and weaknesses would he address?**

Next, ask students, **"What is the most beautiful place you have ever visited?"** (Allow time for student response.) **"What is one of the ugliest places you have seen?"** (Be prepared for all kinds of wild answers, including your own town for the ugliest.)

Bring out some photographs or postcards of the most scenic vacation spot you have visited or would like to visit. Next, show pictures or tell students about one of the dumpiest places you have visited. Conclude this activity by saying, **"John wrote the book of Revelation from Patmos, which evidently was a tiny little island, not much to write or speak about. It wasn't some paradise. Patmos sat forty miles off the southwest coast of present-day Turkey. It was a place where criminals were sent. It was more like Alcatraz than it was Hawaii. Many scholars believe John was sent there for eighteen months, and during this time he wrote Revelation. Let's dig into what John has to say to us."**

LOOKING DEEPER

REVELATION 1:1-6

The book of Revelation points to Jesus Christ as the main character of the book. An angel brought the message to John through signs and symbols. The secondary purpose of Revelation is to show what events "must soon take place" (v. 1). Revelation is the only book that specifically promises a "blessing" to those who read it, hear it and heed it. Since we gain a blessing by reading Revelation, let's enjoy it!

A welcome is given, which is customary in letter writing. It is from "Jesus Christ, who is the faithful witness, the firstborn from the dead, and the ruler of the kings of the earth." Jesus is referred to as the One "who loves us and has freed us from our sins by his blood." Only God can forgive and cleanse sin. John is making reference not just to his Gentile hearers, but also his Jewish audience who understood that a blood sacrifice is the only way to make atonement for sin (Exodus 12:12-14; Leviticus 17:11).

God is making us a kingdom of priests, which means that we can go before the throne of God with free access. In the Old Testament the only persons able to approach God were the priests. The priests prayed and confessed to God their own sins as well as those of the people. Now through the blood covenant of Jesus, we all can make our way into the Holy of Holies. The kingdom means the "rule of God"; therefore, John is saying that those who submit their lives to the rule and reign of God are free to come before him in prayer.

1:7, 8

John describes Jesus as "riding the clouds" (THE MESSAGE). Daniel 7:13 describes the Messiah's return in the same manner: "In my vision at night I looked, and there before me was one like a son of man, coming with the clouds of heaven." In Old Testament imagery, clouds meant divine activity. At the first coming of Christ, few saw his beginning on earth as an infant, but his second coming will be open for all to see.

Names are vital in the Bible, for they describe one's attributes and personalities. Jesus is Alpha and Omega, the first and last letters of the Greek alphabet. Nothing was before Jesus and nothing will outlive him. As God, he is denoted as past, present and future.

1:9-11

On the Lord's Day, or Sunday, the apostle John received a vision of Jesus and was told to write to seven churches. He was on the island of Patmos in the Aegean Sea, banished there because he would not reject his Christianity. Patmos was a six-by-ten-mile island. Criminals were banished to Patmos, so this place probably didn't print nice postcards! John heard a sound like a loud trumpet. Somehow he was transported to a heavenly scene, telling him to record in a scroll what he saw and to send these letters to seven churches in western Asia Minor, which were located closely to one another.

1:12-19

In the vision, John sees Jesus glorified. John had seen Jesus many times healing people, working miracles, giving sight to the blind, feeding the hungry and changing lives—but this encounter was radically different! This visitation of Jesus caused John to faint as though he were dead! John worshiped Jesus facedown. In his book, *When Christ Comes*, Max Lucado writes, "Keep in mind that what John wrote is not what he saw. . . . What he wrote is like what he saw. But what he saw was so otherworldly that he had no words to describe it."[2]

Check This . . .

If possible, never teach or lead Sunday school, youth group or small groups alone. Have another adult helper.

Check This . . .

Why were there seven churches? In his study guide called *Letters to Churches*, Chuck Swindoll adds these insights:

• Geographically, the location of these churches made them readily accessible to one another and the world.

• Historically, these churches exemplified strengths Jesus wanted to commend, and, except in Smyrna's and Philadelphia's cases, problems he wanted to correct.

• Spiritually, churches of every age share the same strengths and weaknesses as the seven churches.[1]

John used images, symbols to draw out what Christ looked like to him. He used word pictures to describe the indescribable. John used words that most students like to use, such as "like." "Like" is the word John used to describe the risen Lord. Hair like wool, feet like bronze, eyes like fire, a voice like rushing water. John stated that Jesus looked like the sun shining at the brightest time of the day!

John tried to communicate a vision that was almost impossible to explain, similar to describing a sunset to a blind person. The long robe and golden sash around Jesus' chest signified the wardrobe of the high priest. Jesus is not just any priest. Hebrew 7:26 states, "So now we have a high priest who perfectly fits our needs: completely holy, uncompromised by sin, with authority extending as high as God's presence in heaven itself" (THE MESSAGE).

Verse fourteen says, "His head and hair were white like wool, as white as snow." Daniel 7:9 speaks of God as the "Ancient of Days," whose clothing was "as white as snow; the hair of his head was white like wool." This description speaks to the eternal existence of Jesus, and the concept of white wool and snow points to his purity. John's vision was of the spotless Lamb of God!

His eyes were like a flame of fire. Moses saw a burning bush, Daniel saw a fiery furnace, but John saw eyes on fire. These were eyes that could pierce one's soul. Both feet were like furnace-fired bronze. Daniel 10:6 describes "eyes like flaming torches" and "arms and legs like the gleam of burnished bronze." Bronze speaks of great power. In his book, *Reversed Thunder*, Eugene Peterson explains this metal:

"Bronze is a combination of iron and copper. Iron is strong but it rusts. Copper won't rust but it's pliable. Combine the two in bronze and the best quality of each is preserved, the strength of the iron and the endurance of the copper. The rule of Christ is set on this base: the foundation is tested by fire."[3]

His voice must have been like the sound of powerful waters like Niagara Falls or some majestic waterfalls in Hawaii. The glory of God is spectacular. Jesus' voice will be ever-present in Heaven—strong and steady, yet soothing and riveting. He held in his right hand seven stars, which are the leaders of the seven churches. The right hand is a sign of readiness to get moving. And, coming from his mouth was a two-edged sword, a tongue-shaped sword for close fighting. His face was shining like the sun. Heaven will be a place of brightness and light, radiating from the throne of God.

1:20

John was commanded to record what he saw plus that which would be revealed to him later. The message was to be delivered to the seven lampstands, or seven churches, and the messengers are called "angels." This term has been widely debated. It is hard to comprehend how an angelic being could carry the mail to the churches. Many scholars believe the term angel comes from the Greek word meaning "messenger"; therefore, it seems most likely this is directed to the core leadership of each Christian gathering or the "spirit" of the leadership of that particular community of Christ.

LASER SURGERY

1. SEVEN CHURCHES/ SEVEN YOUTH GROUPS

Ahead of time, photocopy the student sheet on page 16 of this book onto a transparency. Ask everyone to break into groups of two to four. Distribute writing utensils and copies of the student sheet. Make sure each group has at least one Bible. Assign a specific church and Scripture to each group, asking them to identify strengths and weaknesses of their assigned church. If you are dealing with ten students or less, have them pair up and take two of the churches.

Give students about five minutes to read their Scriptures, then invite one person from each group to record the praises and problems of each church. Volunteers from each group can write their answers on the transparency.

Next, have students take turns reading Revelation 1. Explain the background using some of the information in the introduction of this book as well as the Bible commentary. Finally, brainstorm how your group is similar to any of these seven churches.

2. JUST A GLIMPSE OF JESUS

Ask students, **"What do you think Jesus looked like when he was on earth? Describe his looks, his characteristics."**

After students have responded, display various pictures of Jesus, including pictures from children's books, photographs from a movie about Jesus, etc. Then ask, **"What do you think he looks like now in Heaven?"** Allow students to respond, then take a look at his description in Revelation 1:13-16.

Distribute drawing paper and markers and ask students to draw a picture of the glorified Jesus. After they have finished and shown their pictures to one another, comment, **"Our pictures can't possibly do justice to how incredible Jesus really is. And, the awesome thing is that he's not just the Jesus of the past, or of the future—he's the Jesus of today. Let's see what he has to say to us today."**

Materials needed:
Reproducible student sheet on page 16 of this book; Bibles; writing utensils; transparency; overhead projector

Check This . . .

It's a good idea to allow students to give leadership. Involve several students in reading Revelation 1 aloud. When they have finished, tell students that Revelation 1:3 is the only place in the Bible that says they get a blessing from God just by reading Revelation. And this involves simple ideas like having someone in charge of starting and stopping the video clips.

Materials needed:
Pictures of Jesus; Bible; drawing paper; markers

Extra Options . . .

- Christ has promised that he will return again. What steps do we need to take to be ready? (See John 14:1-3; Matthew 24:27-31; Revelation 19:11-16, 19-21.)
- Jesus still forgives sin. What places of your life need some clean-up?
- Jesus wants to be in the center of our youth group. What can we do to make him feel at home?
- The resurrected, ascended Jesus is awesome and majestic (vv. 12-18). Why is worship important?

GETTING FOCUSED

1. W.W.J.S. (WHAT WOULD JESUS SAY?)

Materials needed:
Blank paper; writing utensils

Distribute blank paper and writing utensils to students. Begin by sharing some of the descriptions concerning Jesus in Revelation 1:

- **"His voice was like the sound of rushing waters." What does Christ want to say to you personally today?**
- **"His face was like the sun shining in all its brilliance." What vision does Christ want to give you?**
- **"His eyes were like blazing fire." What sin is Christ telling you needs to go?**

Ask students to write a letter to themselves based on these three questions, as if Jesus were writing to them personally. What strengths would Jesus say they possess? How about weaknesses? Allow students five to eight minutes to write their letters. Encourage them to take their letters home and put them in a place where they'll remember to pull them out at the end of this study of Revelation. Close in prayer.

2. SEEKING STRENGTH

Materials needed:
Reproducible student sheet on page 16 of this book; transparency; overhead projector

Reread some of the strengths of the seven churches that students recorded earlier on the transparency. Then, ask students to identify which church seems most like their youth group. Encourage them to discuss these questions:

- **What are some ways that our youth group may have gotten off track with loving Jesus first?**
- **What are some ways to get back on track with loving him first?**

Ask your group to pray silently, and ask God to help them practice one of the strengths this week. For example, when thinking about the strength, "I know you are a hard worker," they would pray to overcome spiritual laziness in their prayer life. Then read one or two of the weaknesses of the churches. As you read a few, have them close their eyes and listen. Read them over again, and in their silent prayers, have students identify one of these problems they need to work on this week.

Agree or Disagree?

1   Red hair is weird.

2   The end of the world is right around the corner.

3   Abortion is always wrong.

4   Being the President of the United States is the toughest job one could have.

5   Michael Jordan is the greatest athlete of all time.

6   The second coming of Christ won't take place anytime soon.

7 Churches
seven
Seven Youth Groups

The church of Ephesus was a hardworking group of believers who possessed the endurance and stamina necessary for stressful times, but their spiritual dynamism was lacking. They had left their first love—their love for God.

The church of Smyrna was busy doing spiritual warfare and was encouraged to be brave and bold in their fight. No rebukes.

The believers at Pergamum were applauded for speaking out in the name of the Lord, but severely rebuked for giving into temptation.

The church of Thyatira was strong in faith, love and service, yet had allowed false teachings to emerge in their church.

The saints at Sardis had a reputation for being alive, but they were in reality spiritually dead. These people were the walking dead.

The believers at Philadelphia were a small group of Christians but they were mighty in the Spirit of God! No corrections made.

The church of Laodicea had become spiritually stale and therefore severely admonished by Jesus. They had become lukewarm and stagnant.

Five of the churches were given some kind of corrective words—all except Smyrna and Philadelphia.

Church	Scripture	Praises	Problems
Ephesus	2:1-7		
Smyrna	2:8-11		
Pergamum	2:12-17		
Thyatira	2:18-29		
Sardis	3:1-6		
Philadelphia	3:7-13		
Laodicea	3:14-20		
Our youth group			

LET THE MAIN THING BE THE MAIN THING

If there's any topic your students think they know a lot about, it's this—love. As you introduce the idea of "leaving your first love," many students will be able to relate to something they once loved, then later realized they no longer cared for. Some students may have received a "Dear John" letter in which a girlfriend or boyfriend broke up with them. They will understand what it means to have lost at love.

In today's study, your students will have the opportunity to talk about love, although it might not be the kind of love they're used to discussing. The church of Ephesus had abandoned their first love. In his love letter to this church, Jesus gets to the heart of the matter.

EYE-POPPING OPENERS

1. VIDEO INTERVIEWS

The week before this lesson, take a handful of students and interview some people about the second coming of Christ. Some possible questions to ask those they interview include:

- **Are you afraid of the future?**
- **Are we living in the end times?**
- **Do you believe that Jesus Christ will literally come again?**
- **If yes, do you feel it will be soon? Why or why not?**
- **What word describes how you feel about Christ's return: excitement, fear, confusion, worry, doubt?**

Begin this session by showing the video to your students. Remind them about the vision that John had concerning what he was to say to the seven churches. Then comment, **"Today, we will take a look at what Jesus had to say to the church at Ephesus."**

2. LOVE 'EM AND LEAVE 'EM

Begin this activity by telling the following story:

"Andrew used to really like Jennifer—a lot. But over the past few weeks he just doesn't seem to be excited about being with her. The feelings he used to have seem to be gone. He says he still loves her and would like to marry her someday. They are both seniors in high school and are planning to go to the same college. Jennifer is convinced that Andrew is 'the only one' for her—she is certain that God has brought them together. She is committed to Andrew, yet she senses that Andrew is becoming

---

LESSON TEXT
Revelation 2:1-7

LESSON FOCUS
Ephesus was a prominent church but had left behind the most important ingredient—love for Christ.

LESSON GOALS
As result of participating in this lesson, students will:
- Learn strengths and weaknesses of the Ephesian church.
- Determine some ways to avoid spiritual backsliding.
- Develop some tactics for making their youth group successful.

Materials needed:
Video recorder; blank videotape; VCR and monitor

Media Moment
Play the song "People Get Ready," by Crystal Lewis, "Come Quickly Lord," by Rebecca St. James, or "I Wish We'd All Been Ready," by dc Talk, from the compilation album *People Get Ready*.

distant from her. In fact, Andrew is beginning to make excuses about why he cannot get together with her on dates."

After you have read the story, ask students to respond to these questions:

- **What advice would you give Andrew?**
- **What advice would you give Jennifer?**
- **Have you ever loved something, even as a little kid, and then realized one day that you didn't love it anymore? What happened?**
- **Have you ever received a love letter or a "Dear John" letter (otherwise known as a "Let's just be friends" letter)? How did you respond to the letter?**

Conclude by saying, **"In our study today we're going to look at a church that had lost its first love."**

LOOKING DEEPER

The city of Ephesus is mentioned first in John's vision probably because it was the greatest harbor in Asia and was considered one of the top three cities of the eastern Mediterranean. It was known as the Supreme Metropolis of Asia. Ephesus was a wealthy city with sea trade; politically it was the home of the Roman governor and a hub for important trials. It was also home to the Athenian Games. Spiritually, Ephesus was the center of the worship of the goddess Diana, or Artemis, which essentially was a cult of prostitution. The statue of Artemis was considered one of the seven ancient wonders of the world; therefore, Ephesus had lots of activity and visitors! Jews, Greeks, criminals and prostitutes lived there. According to Acts 18, the church of Ephesus was probably founded by the apostle Paul, along with Priscilla and Aquila. Paul stayed in Ephesus for three years on his third journey, teaching and doing ministry (Acts 20:29-31).

REVELATION 2:1-3

With any love letter, there is typically some affirmation and also when needed, some brutal honesty. Often this includes some rebuke and then some ideas for implementing change. This is exactly the pattern of the seven letters: five churches received encouragement. Sardis and Laodicea received only correction, no affirmation. Smyrna and Philadelphia received only praise. The goal for all seven was for healing and restoration.

The letter was addressed to the attention of "the angel" (or better translated "messenger") of the church—probably one of the main teaching elders of the congregation. The spokesperson is the resurrected Jesus. He proceeds to give some strengths and weaknesses of the church of Ephesus. "I know," Jesus says, meaning that he is intimately aware of the way they are wired. These believers were hard workers. They had endured hardships and had not thrown in the towel. They were reaching out to others, energetic and enthusiastic.

They were also applauded for being strong in teaching and keeping heresy away from the people of God. ("Heresy" is teaching that deviates from mainstream biblical Christianity.)

2:4

Next, Jesus zooms in with his eyes of fire to point out one noticeable problem. In fact, it is a huge temptation for all youth groups. "I hold this against you: You have forsaken your first love." Their intensity, priority and passion for Jesus had become insignificant. It is so easy to put things, cars, dating, sports and materialism ahead of God. To "leave" something generally happens over a period of time. Erosion doesn't happen overnight; it takes time to leave something, such as a man leaving his wife, or a college student deciding to quit school. It also takes time to learn to love. The church had become distant in their love for Christ. Their "first" love had faded. Not lost it, just left it. Perhaps this church had gotten a little slack about the return of Christ. Maybe they didn't take it seriously or weren't anticipating his coming.

2:5-7

Jesus doesn't leave the church hanging hopelessly. He offers words of hope and words to enable change—remember, do and hear. These are active words.

The Ephesian church had stepped to the plate in guarding the truth, and steered clear of false teachers, but they were striking out when it came to love. They loved knowledge of God, but forgot what's most important—loving God and others. Somehow they forgot Jesus, their first love, and the return of Christ was the farthest concept from their hearts and minds. Jesus sends words to this church on how to get back in the game.

LASER SURGERY

1. YOUR FIRST LOVE

Distribute writing utensils and copies of the student sheet on page 23 of this book. Allow students to break into groups of three or four, according to the number of pets that they "love." Make sure each group has at least one Bible. Ask students to read Revelation 2:1-7 in their groups, then give them ten minutes to answer the questions found on the student sheet. Refer to the **Looking Deeper** section to provide necessary background information.

After students have completed their work, comment, **"Often, the reward of loving someone in a relationship is receiving their love in return. To those who passionately pursue Jesus, he promises an eternity spent with him, eating from the tree of life. It just doesn't get any better than that."**

Materials needed:
Reproducible student sheet on page 23 of this book; Bibles; writing utensils

2. WHAT'S A YOUTH GROUP TO DO?

Materials needed:
Bible; chalkboard and chalk or markerboard and marker

Extra Options . . .

- What the Bible says about the role of angels (see Genesis 16:7-12; Exodus 14:19; 2 Samuel 24:16; Ezekiel 1:4-14; Daniel 6:22; Luke 1:26-28; Revelation 5:11, 12; 12:7-9; 20:1, 2).
- What the Bible says about the second coming of Christ.
- What is distracting our youth group away from Jesus? Are we in need of spiritual refueling?
- Jesus comes again with flames of fire in his eyes. How will you respond to his coming?

Ask a good reader to read aloud Revelation 2:5-7. Then, write on the board these three words in bold letters: **Remember, Do** and **Hear.** Draw a vertical line between each of these words, from the top of the board to the bottom.

Say, **"Jesus doesn't give us a warning and then leave it to us to try and figure out how to turn it around. He lays out three specific steps that anyone or any group can take to recapture their first love. Jesus asks the church of Ephesus (and us), 'Do you have any idea how far you've fallen?' The first step on the road to restoring a love relationship with Jesus is to remember how things used to be. The first step of a dying marriage is to restore the romance, to remember the honeymoon days. The first step of getting new energy for school or a job is to recall the first moments of excitement you once had. Coming back to the Father is all about remembering. Remember what it was like when you first accepted Jesus? How excited you were? How you wanted to read his word and talk to him? You can start over, make an about-face and come clean before God."**

Ask students:

- **Can you think of a time when our youth group was more focused on God? How have we become distracted?** Record their responses under the word, "Remember."

Continue by saying, **"Next, Jesus says, 'Do the things you did at first.' Does our youth group need to recover something in our love for Jesus that might have been replaced with other stuff? The Ephesians were told to do the deeds they first did. Jesus is challenging his hearers to do an about-face toward him. Do a 180! In other words, fall in love all over again!"**

Ask students:

- **What might Jesus have in mind for our group? Bible studies, more prayer time, service projects? Maybe we need to consider what we are *not* doing.** Record their responses under the word, "Do."

Continue, **"Finally, Jesus challenges us with these words, as paraphrased in THE MESSAGE: 'Are your ears awake? Listen. Listen to the Wind Words, the Spirit blowing through the churches.' Listening might be the hardest discipline in life. When it comes to spiritual disciplines, listening to God is by far the most difficult and maybe the least practiced. Some of us have selective hearing skills—we hear what we want to hear and let the rest go right in and out of our ears."**

Ask students:

- **How can we do a better job of listening to God?** Record their responses under the word, "Hear."

Conclude this activity by asking, **"Is the Spirit of God saying to us, 'Do you love me like you used to? Have you let your love for**

God slip into other areas like sports, friends, love relationships or popularity?' Come back to me today."

GETTING FOCUSED

1. THE KISS

Before class, tape a long piece of butcher paper to the classroom wall. Begin this activity by reading the following:

"In his book *Mortal Lessons*, physician Richard Selzer describes a scene in a hospital room after he had performed surgery on the face of a young woman:

'I stand by the bed where the young woman lies . . . her face, postoperative . . . her mouth twisted in palsy . . . clownish. A tiny twig of the facial nerve, one of the muscles of her mouth, has been severed. She will be that way from now on. I had followed with religious fervor the curve of her flesh, I promise you that. Nevertheless, to remove the tumor in her cheek, I had cut this little nerve. Her young husband is in the room. He stands on the opposite side of the bed, and together they seem to be in a world all their own in the evening lamplight . . . isolated from me . . . private.

'Who are they? I ask myself . . . he and this wry mouth I have made, who gaze at and touch each other so generously. The young woman speaks. "Will my mouth always be like this?" she asks. "Yes," I say, "it will. It is because the nerve was cut." She nods and is silent. But the young man smiles. "I like it," he says. "It's kind of cute."

'All at once I know who he is. I understand, and I lower my gaze. One is not bold in an encounter with the living. Unmindful, he bends to kiss her crooked mouth, and I am so close I can see how he twists his own lips to accommodate to hers . . . to show her that their kiss still works.'"[1]

After you have read this story, ask students to list on a piece of butcher paper all the activities their youth group does during the year—everything. Then go through the list and ask students these questions:

- **Which of these activities brings you closer to Jesus?**
- **Which of these things has no real lasting impact on your intimacy with Jesus?**
- **In what ways has our group "left our first love" like the Ephesian church did?**

Help students evaluate how much of their time is being spent on things that essentially have little or no bearing on their walk with God.

Materials needed:
Butcher paper; masking tape; markers

Materials needed:
Reproducible student sheet on page 24 of this book; Bibles; writing utensils

Media Moment

A great worship song to close with is "The Heart of Worship," by Matt Redmond. It is recorded on the *Better Is One Day* Passion CD.

2. ARE YOU READY?

Begin by saying, **"As we discussed at the beginning of this lesson, when people think about the return of Christ, they have a variety of emotions including excitement, fear, confusion, worry and doubt. The way they feel probably has to do with whether or not they are ready for him to return. What about you? How do you feel about the future? Are you ready? Let's take a look at some Scriptures that should help us be more prepared."**

Distribute writing utensils and copies of the student sheet on page 24 of this book. Make sure students have Bibles. Give sufficient time to complete the sheet. If you run out of time, encourage students to finish looking up the Scriptures at home. In each instance, students are to write down any observations, insights or warnings found in God's Word.

Close in prayer, asking God to help students return to their first love.

Your First Love

Read Revelation 2:1-7. Then answer the questions that follow:

I,ve Got Good News!

- What are the positive qualities (strengths) that Jesus says are true of the Christians at Ephesus?

- What are some positive characteristics (strengths) of our group?

I,ve Got Bad News!

- What is the only negative statement Jesus has to say about the Ephesian church?

- How important or unimportant do you think this one issue is compared to all the great stuff happening in the Ephesian church? Why?

- What are some negative characteristics (weaknesses) of our group?

- Which of these is the most serious? Why?

- Have you ever been "in love"? How did you spend your time? What is Jesus saying to us?

- What is the danger in doing and believing the "right" things and yet forgetting why you were doing them in the first place?

- What does Jesus want from us? What's the reward for those who listen to the instructions of Jesus? (v. 7)

ARE YOU READY?

When Jesus returns to the earth, it is going to be so incredible we cannot begin to imagine what it will be like. In the chart below, look up the following Scripture verses, then list any observations, warnings or insights you discover.

Scripture	Observations	Warnings	Insights
Revelation 1:7 _How will Christ come?_			
Matthew 24:1-14 _What are some of the signs of his coming?_			
Acts 1:10, 11 _How will Jesus return?_			
Matthew 24:36-44 _How should we be prepared?_			
1 Thessalonians 4:13-18 _Who will be raised with Christ?_			
1 Thessalonians 5:1-11 _What should our response be to the coming of Christ?_			
Revelation 19:11-21 _What will Christ do when he returns?_			
Revelation 2:4-7 _How should we get ready?_			

WHEN THE GOING GETS TOUGH

Often, we don't find out what we're made of until trouble comes. It may be in the form of sickness, suffering, persecution or just the day-to-day living in the real world. It may affect us or the friends and family connected with us. But, it *will* come. In today's study, your students will hear the words Jesus spoke to two more of the churches of Asia, the churches of Smyrna and Pergamum. Both of them were living on Satan's turf and it would take everything in them to stand firm until the end.

EYE-POPPING OPENERS

1. AFFIRMATION GRAFFITI

As students enter, give each person a blank piece of paper and something to write with. Ask students to tape the papers to one another's backs. After all of the students have arrived, begin by saying, **"Some of us may have had a tough week. Today we're going to begin by encouraging one another. On my signal I want you to go around the room and write something on the back of every other person. You need to write something positive, such as, 'You are funny,' 'You have a great smile' or 'You really love God.' Ready? Go!"**

After everyone has had a chance to write something on the back of every other person, let students take the papers off and look at them. Encourage them to take the graffiti home as a source of encouragement.

Conclude this activity by saying, **"As we continue our study of the seven churches in Revelation, we're going to look at a church who was affirmed by Jesus for overcoming Satan and handling suffering."**

2. THE STAIN OF SIN

After students have arrived, draw their attention to the glass of water you are holding in your hand. Talk about how pure it is, with the exception of the chemicals from the tap. Show a gallon of pure drinking water, the kind that is drawn from a stream with no added chemicals.

Comment, **"When we were born, we were created like this— pure and without sin. But something happened to us. Sin entered our world and our lives.** (Place a single drop of dark food coloring in the glass of water.) **Watch how it permeates the entire glass.** (Add another drop of food coloring.) **See how few drops it takes to darken all the pure water? Because of sin, that is exactly the condition of our hearts without the cleansing impact of**

LESSON TEXT
Revelation 2:8-17

LESSON FOCUS
Two churches faced different struggles—suffering for one and sin for the other.

LESSON GOALS
As a result of participating in this lesson, students will:
- Realize some steps they can take to handle tough times in their lives.
- Celebrate some promises God has given them.
- Discover the consequences and some remedies for sin.
- Understand the reality of Satan.

Materials needed:
Blank paper; masking tape; writing utensils that don't bleed through paper

Media Moment

Show the opening scene of *The Mission* with Robert DeNiro. The clip runs from 00:35 to 4:16 and depicts a martyred Jesuit priest bound to a cross, and placed in the rapids where he plunges 200 feet down a waterfall. The story is about a soldier and slave trader who murders his brother, then eventually becomes a priest. After the clip, ask students:
- **Is suffering normal for a Christian?**
- **Why do we want to avoid suffering and persecution?**
- **What price should we have to pay to be a follower of Jesus?**

25

Materials needed:
Glass; gallon of water; eyedropper; food coloring

Christ. As we continue our study of the seven churches of Revelation, today we're going to see how a little sin goes a long way and affects the whole. Jesus had some strong words of correction for one of the churches who had been greatly affected by sin. Let's take a deeper look."

LOOKING DEEPER

REVELATION 2:8

Smyrna, which means "myrrh" or perfume, was considered the "first of Asia" because of its beauty. The city was known for its excellent harbor, commerce, public theaters, lavish temples and famous stadium. It was a beautiful town surrounded by the foothills of Mt. Pagos, five hundred feet above the port. Heathen cultures and religions were embedded in Smyrna as evidenced by temples to Aphrodite and the worship of the "gods" Zeus, Apollo and Mercury. Smyrna was a center for emperor and pagan worship. Christians were not popular in Smyrna—they were harassed and persecuted—and many mass executions occurred for those who refused to worship the emperor. Smyrna was eventually destroyed by an earthquake in A.D. 177.

Smyrna is one of only two churches for which Jesus had no corrective words. The Lord Jesus used the phrase "the First and the Last" to communicate that he is the beginning and the end, the "alpha and omega," which are the first and last words of the Greek alphabet. He is the beginning of life and the end of life. He "died and came to life again." Jesus is telling the believers of Smyrna that he has given them resurrection power to survive and thrive in a pagan world.

2:9-11

The word John uses for tribulation paints a word picture of a rock that crushes anything underneath it, and the Christians at Smyrna were being crushed. When Jesus tells them they are rich, he is not referring to materialistic possessions, but spiritual wealth that cannot be bought. Many of the church at Smyrna must have been either slaves or of the low class. There were some Jewish antagonists referred to as "a synagogue of Satan," who were harassing these believers. This is the first mention of Satan in the book of Revelation.

Since being a Christian was illegal, some of the believers had their homes and businesses ransacked; therefore, they were dirt poor. Some were imprisoned and that usually led to death. Yet Jesus offers encouragement and hope. The believers of Smyrna were not to be afraid, but rather be faithful—"even to the point of death." If they stood tall, they would receive the crown of life.

On February 23, A.D. 155, Polycarp of Smyrna was martyred for his faith. The proconsul told Polycarp to choose Caesar as Lord or Jesus as Lord. Polycarp said, "Eighty and six years have I served Him . . . and He has done me no wrong. How can I blaspheme my King who saved me?" The proconsul threatened him with burning, and Polycarp replied, "You threaten me with the fire that burns for a time, and is quickly quenched, for you do not know the fire which awaits the wicked in the judgment to come and in everlasting punishment."

Polycarp was burned alive. Killed for his faith.

2:12, 13

Pergamum was a very wealthy city. It did not have the great roads like Smyrna or Ephesus, but by the time John wrote this letter, Pergamum had been a capital city for 400 years. It was built on a tall hill, so you could see the Mediterranean fifteen miles away. It was the heart of Caesar worship, so to be a Christian in Pergamum was a difficult challenge. There were many temples and altars to Zeus, Athena and Dionysus. As in Smyrna, emperor worship was ever-present and believers in Jesus were in danger of losing their lives.

John communicates to these believers that Jesus is the One who "has the sharp, double-edged sword," a reference to the power of God's word. Jesus is telling these Christians, "I know that you live in Satan's turf, but I have given you the power to overcome."

Antipas was a Christian, who, according to tradition was roasted to death in a brazen bull. The word "witness" Jesus calls him can also be translated "martyr"—one who loses his life for Christ. To be a witness for Christ involves living for Christ and yes, being willing to die for Christ.

2:14, 15

Jesus has a few rebukes for this church. Balaam was a man who after being prevented from cursing Israel, advised Balak, king of Moab, that the Israelites would forfeit God's protection if he could induce them to worship idols (see Numbers 25, 31). This incident became proverbial for spiritual backsliding.

THE MESSAGE paraphrases in these words: "Don't you remember that Balaam was an enemy agent, seducing Balak and sabotaging Israel's holy pilgrimage by throwing unholy parties?" It was all about compromise, trying to fit in with the culture. The believers in Pergamum had also fallen into some teaching by the Nicolaitans, who were like Balaam, accommodating themselves to their culture.

2:16, 17

Christ gives them a hard and fast word: "Repent." It is a word that means to turn around, about-face, get moving in a new direction. To those who change and overcome they are promised "some of the hidden manna" and "a white stone with a new name written on it." The image of manna is a reference to the supernatural feeding the Israelites received from God during their wilderness wanderings (Exodus 16:14, 15). Jesus is telling the church that if they will overcome worldly seduction, he will provide for them in unique ways.

The white stone is possibly a reference to ancient law in which an individual was forgiven by a jury. The jurors would drop a white stone into an urn to signify the person had been acquitted. Jesus is promising forgiveness for the believers at Pergamum. A new name means a new identity or new beginning. Just as Abram became Abraham and Jacob became Israel, the church at Pergamum will get a new name in Heaven—as will we!

LASER SURGERY

1. WHAT ON EARTH IS SATAN DOING?

Materials needed:
Reproducible student sheet on page 31 of this book; Bibles; writing utensils

Begin by reading Revelation 2:8-17 aloud, allowing several students to each read a verse. Share some of the background information concerning the cities and churches of Smyrna and Pergamum from the **Looking Deeper** section. Then point out the phrases, "a synagogue of Satan" (v. 9), "the devil will put some of you in prison to test you" (v. 10), "where Satan has his throne" and "where Satan lives" (v. 13). Comment, **"Looks like Satan was as active in those days as he is today. Let's see what we can find out about his evil work."**

Ask students these questions:

- **What Satanic influences have you seen in our town?**
- **What are some places that seem to be "Satan's turf"?**

Allow students to break into groups of three to five people. Distribute writing utensils and copies of the student sheet on page 31 of this book. Make sure each small group has at least one Bible. Ask students to look up the Scriptures listed on the sheet and answer the questions they find there.

Conclude by saying, **"I'm glad we know what happens at the end of the book, aren't you? That should give us a reason to stand strong against all the temptations Satan throws our way. We know that ultimately he is the loser!"**

2. REVELATION MAD-LIB

Materials needed:
Bibles; writing utensil

A Mad-Lib is a writing activity in which people fill in blanks in a letter or story that are not the correct words, thereby creating a fictitious piece of writing. Mad-Libs are especially popular with good English students. Ask students to take turns providing you with various words that you will use to fill in the blanks below. WARNING: Only ask for the words you need (in the parentheses); don't read the whole letter until students have filled in all of your blanks.

"**To the church at** _____ **(name of your town), I know your** _____ **(plural noun) and your** _____ **(plural noun), yet you are** _____ **(adjective). Do not be** _____ **(adjective) of what you are about to** _____ **(verb). I tell you, the** _____ **(noun) will put some of you in** _____ **(another noun) to** _____ **(verb) you, and you will suffer** _____ **(noun) for** _____ **(a number)** _____ **and** _____ **(two different days of the week). Be** _____ **(adjective), even to the point of** _____ **(noun) and** _____ **(a famous person) will give you a** _____ **(noun) of** _____ **(noun).**

To the church at _____ (name of a town), these are the
_____ (noun) of him who has the sharp, double-edged
_____ (noun). I know where you _____ (verb)—where
_____ (an evil villain) has his throne. Yet you remain
_____ (adjective) to my _____ (noun). You did not
renounce your _____ (noun) in me, even in the days of
_____ (a person's name) who was put to death in your (same
town as listed above). I have this against you. There are some, name-
ly _____ and _____ (two people from your youth
group) who hold to the teaching of _____ (a musician or a
band), who taught _____ (a friend's name) to entice the
_____ (school mascot) by eating _____ (horrible
food) sacrificed to _____ (zoo animal) and by committing
_____ (a crime). Likewise, some of the _____
(name of a school club) have held on to the teaching of the
_____ (pro football team). _____ (a com-
mand) therefore! Or _____ (a superhero) will come again
soon and will _____ (verb) against
_____ (same school club as above).

He who has an _____ (noun) let him _____ (verb)."

After you have filled in all of the blanks, read the fictitious letter to
the group. Comment, **"This was a made-up letter taken from some
real words in Revelation. We were way off course, weren't we?
What Jesus really said to these churches was no laughing matter.
Let's check out the real deal in Revelation 2:8-17."**

After you have read the Scripture, share some of the background
information in the **Looking Deeper** section so students can see what
was really going on in the churches of Smyrna and Pergamum.

You might want to read the warning found in Revelation 22:18, 19
and remind students that the Mad-Lib is not be taken literally, since we
don't want to reap the plagues described in the book of Revelation.

Extra Options . . .

- The role of Satan in the lives of people today (Isaiah 14:12-15; Ezekiel
28:12-19; John 10:10; 2 Corinthians
4:4; James 4:7; 1 Peter 5:8).
- The impact of suffering on believers
(Romans 5:3-5; 2 Corinthians 4:17,
18; 11:23-29; Philippians 1:29;
1 Peter 4:12-19).
- Will there be rewards for believers in
Heaven? And what are they?
(1 Corinthians 3:10-15; Revelation
2:10, 11).
- Is being a Christian in America too
easy?

GETTING FOCUSED

1. MY PERFECT YOUTH GROUP

Divide students into smaller groups of three to five people, possibly by the color they are wearing. Distribute writing utensils and
copies of the student sheet on page 32 of this book. Begin by saying,
**"It is hard to imagine a church or youth group that is perfect,
because there really isn't such a thing. Take a few minutes in
your small groups to produce a list of all the qualities that would
go into making up the 'perfect youth group,' if one could exist.
Write down anything you can think of including characteristics,
dreams, resources, activities they would participate in, etc."**

After students have completed this exercise, allow a spokesperson
from each group to read its ideas aloud. Then have them list qualities
Jesus would want in his youth group. Contrast any differences.

Materials needed:
Reproducible student sheet on page 32 of this
book; writing utensils

29

Ask students:
- **Are there things we are doing that we should *not* be doing?**
- **Are there things we are *not* doing that we should be doing?**

2. TURN IT AROUND

Read the following true story to your students:

"**On New Year's Day, 1929, Georgia Tech played the University of California in the Rose Bowl. In that game, a UCLA player named Roy Riegels recovered a fumble, but somehow got confused and started running 65 yards in the wrong direction. One of his teammates, Benny Lom, tackled him just before he scored for the opposing team. When California attempted to punt, Tech blocked the kick and scored a safety.**

"**Since that strange play happened in the first half, everyone watching the game was asking the same question: 'What will Coach Nibbs Price do with Roy Riegels in the second half?' The players filed off the field, went into the dressing room and sat down on the benches and the floor—all except Riegels. He put his blanket around his shoulders, sat down in a corner, put his face in his hands and cried like a baby.**

"**A coach usually has a great deal to say to his team during halftime, but that day, Coach Price was quiet. No doubt he was trying to decide what to do with Riegels. Then the timekeeper came in and announced that there were only three minutes till play time. Price looked at the team and said simply, 'Men, the same team that played the first half will start the second.'**

"**The players got up and started out—all but Riegels. He didn't budge. The coach looked back and called to him again; still he didn't move. Coach Price went over to where Riegels sat and said, 'Roy, didn't you hear me? The same team that played the first half will start the second.' Then Roy Riegels looked up, and Price saw that his cheeks were wet with a strong man's tears.**

"'**Coach,' he said, 'I can't do it to save my life. I've ruined you. I've ruined the University of California. I've ruined myself. I couldn't face that crowd in the stadium to save my life.'**

"**Then Coach Price put his hand on Riegels's shoulder and said, 'Roy, get up and go on back. The game is only half over.' And Roy Riegels went back, and those Georgia Tech players will tell you they have never seen a man play football as Roy Riegels did in that second half.**"[1]

After you have finished telling the story, ask students:
- **What did Roy Riegels learn that day about the importance of starting over, doing an about-face?**

Conclude by saying, "**According to the words from Revelation we studied today, for those who overcome the difficulties of this life, they will be remembered not for the way they messed up, not for the sins they committed, but for not giving up—for being faithful to the end. And Jesus promises a new name in Heaven, not 'Wrong Way Riegels' (or whatever your last name is) but 'Right Way Riegels.' Hang in there. It's worth it!**"

WHAT ON EARTH IS SATAN DOING?

SATAN WAS AS ALIVE IN THOSE DAYS AS HE IS TODAY!

According to Ephesians 6:10-12, what kind of battle are we in?

What do we know of Satan's history from Ezekiel 28:12-18?

What does the Bible say about Satan's fall? (Isaiah 14:12-14)

What is Satan's main objective? (John 10:10)

What names are given to Satan? (1 Peter 5:8, 9; John 8:44)

Where is the primary battleground we fight Satan? (2 Corinthians 10:3-5)

According to Matthew 4:1-10, how did Jesus defeat Satan?

How did Satan attack the church of Smyrna? (Revelation 2:9)

How was the church of Smyrna to defeat Satan? (2:9, 10)

Revelation 2:13 provides the church of Pergamum a strategy to overcome Satan. What is it?

What happens to Satan in the end? (Revelation 20:7-10)

My Perfect YOUTH GROUP

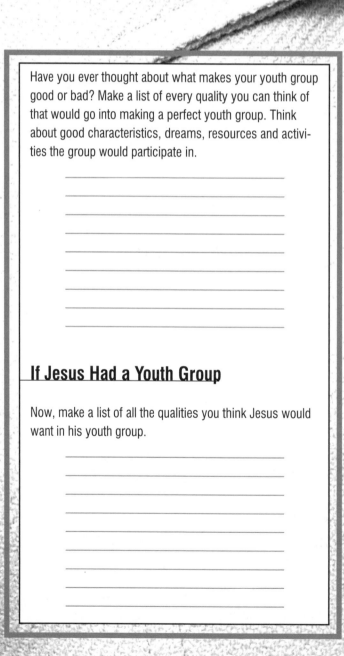

Have you ever thought about what makes your youth group good or bad? Make a list of every quality you can think of that would go into making a perfect youth group. Think about good characteristics, dreams, resources and activities the group would participate in.

_____

_____

_____

_____

_____

_____

_____

_____

_____

_____

_____

If Jesus Had a Youth Group

Now, make a list of all the qualities you think Jesus would want in his youth group.

_____

_____

_____

_____

_____

_____

_____

_____

_____

THE CURE FOR SPIRITUAL CANCER

Cancer. The very sound of the word brings to mind images of suffering and dying—a slow and often painful death. Many of your students have been touched by the lingering effects of cancer as it has stricken someone in their family. Sometimes the cancer could have been treated if it had only been detected earlier. It is the same with spiritual cancer. A problem that may seem small at the time, if left to fester, can escalate into a full-blown spiritual problem. Such was the case with the church at Thyatira. Major surgery was required to correct the disease.

EYE-POPPING OPENERS

1. TAKE ME TO YOUR LEADER

Before class, think of some names of leaders who have impacted the world positively and negatively: Adolph Hitler, Christopher Columbus, Joseph Stalin, Martin Luther, Abraham Lincoln, Saddam Hussein, Billy Graham, Mother Teresa, Bill Clinton, etc. Write each of these names on a piece of small poster board.

Begin this activity by inviting a student to come to the front of the room. Make sure your volunteer's back is to the poster board so he or she can't see the names. Choose one of the leaders' names and allow the student to ask only "Yes" and "No" questions about the person. For instance: "Is this person alive?" or "Did this person have a big impact on a world war?" Allow the contestant to ask five questions, then see if he or she can name the leader.

Continue choosing students to try to guess each of the leaders until your list is exhausted or it's time to move on. Award some kind of prize to the winners.

Conclude this activity by saying, **"World leaders can exercise their influence either for good or bad. As we continue in our study of the churches in Revelation, today we're going to look at a church that was led astray by a strong leader. Let's check it out."**

2. ESKIMO WOLF HUNTERS

Share the following information with your students:

"According to tradition, this is how an Eskimo hunter kills a wolf. First, the Eskimo coats his knife blade with animal blood and allows it to freeze. He then adds layer after layer of blood until the blade is completely concealed by the frozen blood.

LESSON TEXT
Revelation 2:18-29

LESSON FOCUS
The church of Thyatira had allowed a spiritual cancer to eat up some of the cells of the body.

LESSON GOALS
As a result of participating in this lesson, students will:
- Understand the strengths and weaknesses of the church at Thyatira.
- Discover how big problems can happen in small places.
- Discuss the ways sin can spread like cancer in a youth group.
- Implement some strategies to help protect their youth group.

Materials needed:
Several small pieces of poster board; marker; candy prizes

Check This . . .

Play a quick game of Jenga® or Pick up Sticks to show how one piece can affect the outcome. One tumble can affect the rest of the game, as sin can in real life.

Media Media Media Media

Moment

Show a clip from *Patch Adams* that begins at 27:45 and ends at 31:02. Patch Adams is a medical student who uses humor and innovation to be a success. Based on a true story, Adams (Robin Williams) gives us a remarkable view of love and service to others. In this clip, Patch appears in the hospital room with children battling cancer. The segment ends with Adams waving good-bye to the kids with his red nose on. Like some in the church at Thyatira, Patch is committed to love and service. Something as small as cheering up these kids was huge in the long run.

Moment

Show the clip from *The Sandlot* where Benny teaches Smalls how to catch and throw a baseball. Begin playing at 18:28 and stop at 21:56. After the clip, ask students:

- **Why couldn't Smalls initially catch a baseball?**
- **Why did Benny help him learn?**
- **How can we encourage someone who knows less than us about a particular topic?**
- **What keeps us from making a difference in others' lives?**

"Next, the hunter fixes his knife in the ground with the blade up. When a wolf follows his sensitive nose to the source of the scent and discovers the bait, he licks it, tasting the fresh frozen blood. He begins to lick faster, more and more vigorously, lapping the blade until the keen edge is bare. Feverishly now, harder and harder, the wolf licks the blade in the cold Arctic night. His craving for blood becomes so great that the wolf does not notice the razor-sharp sting of the naked blade on his own tongue. Nor does he recognize the instant when his insatiable thirst is being satisfied by his own warm blood. His carnivorous appetite continues to crave more until in the morning light, the wolf is found dead on the snow!"[1]

After you have grossed out your students by reading this story, ask them to consider these questions:

- **Why doesn't the wolf detect the dangerous situation it is in?**
- **Are we ever like that? How?**

Conclude this activity by saying, **"This story is an example of how easy it is, even when things seem to be great, to let your guard down. Just as a wolf licks the blood off the blade of the knife until it kills him, sin can be so delicious and addictive that one does not stop. One of the churches to whom Revelation was addressed was also in grave danger but did not know it. Let's take a look."**

LOOKING DEEPER
REVELATION 2:18, 19

The letter to the church of Thyatira is the longest of the seven, which is ironic, because Thyatira was the least important of all the cities Jesus addressed! Thyatira was on a road which connected Pergamum and Sardis and went on to Philadelphia and Smyrna (all seven churches were geographically close).

Thyatira was a great commercial town. It was a center for the wool and dye industry. It was the gateway to Pergamum, the capital of the province. Thyatira had no special religious heritage. It was not a center of either Caesar or Greek worship. The chances of persecution for the Christians was virtually nonexistent in Thyatira. Christians were "free" from suffering, but were vulnerable to letting their guard down.

The letter begins with another title of Jesus, "Son of God." This is the only time this title is mentioned in all of Revelation. Jesus praised this church for a number of areas. These believers were loving, loyal, serving and enduring. Notice the important references to Jesus' eyes ("like blazing fire") and his feet ("like burnished bronze"). We again see the same statement by Jesus to all seven churches—"I know." To Ephesus, "I know your deeds"; to the church of Smyrna, "I know your afflictions"; to Pergamum, "I know where you live"; and to Thyatira, "I know your deeds." Nothing is a surprise to Jesus. He knows what is going on in our lives.

Jesus commended their deeds, their love, faith, service, perseverance and "that you are now doing more than you did at first." Some youth groups start with a bang in the fall, but then a wave of apathy hits and by the spring just about everybody is barely alive spiritually. The church at Thyatira was finishing stronger than it started.

2:20, 21

Even though there were some wonderful things happening at Thyatira, the piercing eyes of Jesus zeroed in on a situation in need of correction. There was some cancer that needed to be cut out. "But I have this against you, that you tolerate the woman Jezebel, who calls herself a prophetess, and she teaches and leads my bond-servants astray, so that they commit acts of immorality and eat things sacrificed to idols. And I gave her time to repent; and she does not want to repent of her immorality" (*NASB*).

Many scholars have debated who this person was, yet many agree that a particular woman had a spirit of Jezebel. "That woman Jezebel" was a reference to Jezebel in the Old Testament, who was the evil wife of King Ahab (see 1 Kings 18, 19). Jezebel introduced Baal worship plus she killed some of the prophets of God. Even in small cities, big sins can happen.

2:22-29

Jesus offered a cure for this cancer. The Lord who "searches hearts and minds" provided the believers of Thyatira several remedies. First, he said to repent. The word means "metamorphosis," a change from one species to another, as a caterpillar changes to a butterfly. From old creature to new creation. Jesus was saying, "Stop your current behavior and start a new way of living." This church battled sexual immorality, and Christians must still battle the problem today. Yet it is clear that God's intent is for sexual purity until marriage. Adultery and premarital sex are condemned in Scripture.

Second, Jesus encouraged the believers to conquer. Hold on to the truth and defend it! Jesus promised that those who decided to live victoriously, those who refused to follow the spirit of Jezebel, would someday rule the nations.

LASER SURGERY

1. A WARNING FROM THE SURGEON GENERAL

Before class, write down on a transparency some of the background information about Thyatira that is found in the **Looking Deeper** section. For instance, you might want to bullet items like this:

- The longest letter to the "least important" city

Materials needed:
Reproducible student sheet on page 38 of this book; Bibles; writing utensils; transparency; overhead projector

- Center for the wool and dye industry
- Not a center of either Caesar or Greek worship
- Christians were "free" from suffering, but vulnerable to letting their guard down
- The only time the title "Son of God" is mentioned in Revelation
- "I know your deeds"

Ask students to gather in smaller groups of three to five people. Distribute writing utensils and copies of the student sheet on page 38 of this book. Make sure each group has at least one Bible. Ask students to read Revelation 2:18-29 in their groups. Display the transparency with the background information. Then, ask students to work through the questions on their student sheets.

After they have completed their work, conclude by saying, **"Have you ever noticed the surgeon general's warning on billboards and magazine ads regarding the dangers of cigarette smoking potentially leading to cancer? It is as though Jesus were the ultimate Surgeon General providing us this warning about spiritual cancer. We would be wise to follow his advice."**

2. NAME THAT SIN-COM

Distribute writing utensils and copies of the student sheet on page 39 of this book. Make sure that students have Bibles. Comment, **"Some of today's current movies, TV sitcoms, soap operas and popular songs closely resemble some of the evil that we see described in the Bible. In our study today we are looking at the church of Thyatira, which sounds like the set of a contemporary 'sin-com.' The star of the show is Jezebel, an incredibly evil woman."**

Encourage students to read Revelation 2:18-29, then identify current songs, TV shows and movies that fit the descriptions of the statements on the student sheet.

After students have finished working through the sheet, allow several volunteers to share their responses to each of the statements. Refer to some of the background information in the **Looking Deeper** section.

Materials needed:
Reproducible student sheet on page 39 of this book; Bibles; writing utensils

Extra Options . . .

- The importance of one person's influence, either for good or bad.
- The problem of sexual immorality in today's culture.
- God's view of premarital sex (see 1 Corinthians 6:18-20; 1 Thessalonians 4:3-8; Hebrews 13:4).

Materials needed:
Blank paper; writing utensils; video camera; blank videotape; VCR and monitor

GETTING FOCUSED

1. LIGHTS, CAMERA, ACTION!

Divide students into groups of two or three and ask them to write a role play concerning what Jesus might say to their youth group today. In other words, ask them to take Jesus' words to Thyatira and put them in a modern context. Give them a piece of paper to jot down their ideas. Encourage groups to use the same outline that John tended to use:

1. Positive affirmation
2. Corrective discipline
3. A motivating promise

After students have prepared their role plays, let each group come to the front and present its skit, while you roll the camera. If you have time at the end of your session, play the videotape. If not, save it for later use.

2. SEEKING FORGIVENESS

Begin this closing activity by saying, **"It's been said, 'All that is necessary for the triumph of evil is for good men to do nothing.' How might this quote apply to the situation in Thyatira?** (Allow students to respond.) **How might this quote apply to us?"**

Distribute a writing utensil and a 3" x 5" card to each student. Ask them to write on one side of their card the sins they have "tolerated" in their own life. Assure them that no one will see this card. On the other side, have them write out the promise found in 1 John 1:9.

Conclude by asking students to spend a few moments of silent prayer, confessing to God and thanking him that he can and does forgive every sin . . . even mine!

Materials needed:
3" x 5" cards; writing utensils; Bibles

A WARNING FROM THE SURGEON GENERAL

In your group, read Revelation 2:18-29.

This is the only letter to the seven churches (or in the whole book for that matter) where Jesus refers to himself as the "Son of God." What significance do you think this has in light of the problem he addresses to the church at Thyatira?

List all the strengths of the church at Thyatira that Jesus mentions in verse 19.

What is it that Christ has against this church? (vv. 20, 21)

Jesus uses the word "tolerate" in verse 20. What does it mean to be "tolerant"? Can tolerance ever go too far?

What do you think our youth group might be tolerating (big or small) that Jesus wants us to change?

Who was Jezebel? (See 1 Kings 16:31; 19:1-3; 21:25.)

After giving her (and her followers) a chance to repent, Jesus condemns this "Jezebel" to a "bed of suffering." Why do you think he uses the word "bed" as part of his description of what her suffering will be?

Jesus ends his letter to Thyatira with a promise to the overcomers. What is the promise?

What do you feel is the most important point of this lesson for our group? What about you, personally?

NAME That SIN·COM

The description we find of the church of Thyatira sounds like it could have taken place on the set of a contemporary "sin-com." The star of the show is Jezebel, an evil, seductive woman. Read Revelation 2:18-29.

In the statements that follow, identify a current song, TV show or movie that fits each particular description.

✦ Name a current movie that portrays an evil, seductive woman.

✦ Name a current pop or rap song that boldly proclaims that sexual intimacy before marriage is okay.

✦ Name a TV sitcom that deals with human suffering.

✦ Name a movie in which someone commits adultery.

✦ Name a TV show in which children die.

✦ Name a song that deals with the church.

✦ Name a popular movie that deals with the reality of Satan.

✦ Name a TV show that depicts people overcoming tough times and living "happily ever after."

✦ Name a current song that deals with some kind of change taking place.

✦ Name a TV show that deals with the importance of listening.

IT'S TIME TO WAKE UP!

It is entirely possible to appear to be very busy "serving the Lord" and yet be spiritually dead. It happens to churches, youth groups and individual believers. Such was the case of the church at Sardis. On the other hand, the church of Philadelphia was one of two for whom Jesus had no words of rebuke. They had not denied their Lord's name in spite of the trials they had faced. They exemplified what it means to stand firm until the end. In this session, students will have the opportunity to evaluate their youth group and see how they are similar to and different from these two churches for whom Jesus had a message.

EYE-POPPING OPENERS

1. MY YOUTH GROUP

Ahead of time you will need to write out the following questions either on an overhead transparency or on a piece of newsprint:

- **What do you like about our youth group?**
- **What would you change about our youth group?**
- **What activities or events would you like to see us do?**
- **What did you hear in the video that rang true about our group, either positive or negative?**
- **What do you think Jesus would say about our youth group's strengths?**
- **Our weaknesses?**
- **How can you tell if a youth group is dying?**

Begin today's session by showing the "Word on the Street" clip from edition #22 of *Edge TV*. This particular segment is called "My Youth Group." It lasts about two and a half minutes.

After you have shown the clip, display the questions you have prepared and ask students to respond. Encourage them to share their thoughts but not to critique others' ideas. Finally, brainstorm the vital life signs of a healthy youth group.

Conclude this activity by saying, **"As we continue our study of the churches of Revelation, today we will look at a church who at one time had been very alive, but was now dead. Let's look at them and see if we can learn anything about ourselves."**

LESSON TEXT
Revelation 3:1-13

LESSON FOCUS
The church at Sardis had a reputation for being alive, but was now dead, while the believers in Philadelphia were small in size but mighty in the Spirit.

LESSON GOALS
As a result of participating in this lesson, students will:
- Discover the various roadblocks to spiritual blindness.
- Strategize some keys to making their youth group come alive.
- Consider how to make the most of their Christian influence.

Materials needed:
TV and VCR; *Edge TV* video, edition #22; transparency and overhead projector or newsprint and marker

Check This . . .

Edge TV is a video magazine. Well worth the money, it comes once a quarter. It can be ordered by calling (800) 616-EDGE, or contact them at P.O. Box 3505, Colorado Springs, CO, 80935-9936.

Materials needed:
Blank videotape; TV and VCR; CD player; appropriate music

Check This . . .

Gather some beautiful photos of fall foliage, scan them and display them on a large screen or mount them and pass them around your group. If your meeting is taking place during the fall, go outside and observe for yourselves. Comment, **"Although these leaves look beautiful and breathtaking, they are actually dying. Soon they will fall off the tree and we will sweep them into piles and set them on fire. Can you think of anything else they are good for?"** Read Jesus' words in John 15:5, 6.

Media Moment

Show a clip from the movie *Awakenings*. Based on a true story, Leonard Lowe (played by Robert DeNiro) has lived with encephalitis and has been in a catatonic stage for over 30 years. One day Leonard miraculously wakes up. It took enormous doses of a drug called L-Dopa to awaken him. The clip begins at counter 46:24 and ends at 50:03. After showing the clip, ask students: **"What will it take to wake us as a youth group? Is there any evidence that we've been asleep?"**

2. SOME KIND OF ZOMBIE

Arrange with several parents ahead of time to allow you to come into your students' bedrooms early on a Saturday morning and wake them up on camera. You may want to bring a second person with you as a sidekick (a sponsor or another student who has a quick mind and witty tongue!).

Begin the session today by showing the video you made. Play some appropriate background music, such as "Wake Up, Little Suzie," by the Everly Brothers *(The Everly Brothers Greatest Hits*, Delta Records, © 1999) or "Some Kind of Zombie," by Audio Adrenaline. After the students have laughed at one another, conclude by saying, **"Some of you look scary when you wake up! You could frighten the dead. As a matter of fact, some of you looked like dead men walking—zombies. As we continue today in our study of Revelation, we're going to discover a church who at one time had been very alive, but was now dead. Let's look at them and see if we can learn anything about ourselves. It might be time for us to wake up!"**

LOOKING DEEPER

Sardis and Philadelphia. One church was active but spiritually dead, the other small but mighty in spiritual power. Sardis was a center for trade, located fifty miles due east of Smyrna. Sardis was a place of great wealth, but was devastated by an earthquake in A.D. 17. The Emperor Tiberius gave money to rebuild the city and helped it regain its splendor and beauty. But morally, it was bankrupt. The Greek historian Herodotus stated that "the inhabitants of Sardis had over the course of many years acquired a reputation for lax moral standards and even open licentiousness."[1]

REVELATION 3:1-3

Jesus begins with a scorching rebuke of spiritual busyness yet deadness. Sardis was slacking and had become spiritually lethargic. In fact, there are no opening words of affirmation for Sardis, only correction. It is as though Jesus makes a funeral announcement: "Sardis is dead." They had a reputation for being alive, but now are like a corpse. They went through the motions of ritual, prayer and programming, but had no life.

THE MESSAGE renders verses 2, 3 like this: "I see right through your work. You have a reputation for vigor and zest, but you're dead, stone dead. Up on your feet! Take a deep breath! Maybe there's life in you yet. But I wouldn't know it by looking at your busywork; nothing of *God's* work has been completed. Your condition is desperate. Think of the gift you once had in your hands, the Message you heard with your ears—grasp it again and turn back to God."

Jesus gives instruction for resuscitation: Wake up, Strengthen what remains, Remember the truth, Keep the truth and Repent. It's like a dying person being told, "Stay with me. Don't close your eyes."

3:4-6

To those "few people" in Sardis who still were walking faithfully with him, Jesus gave three promises:

1. They will walk with him in white—clothed with Christ's righteousness.
2. Their name will remain in the book of life—nothing can separate them from the love of Jesus.
3. Their name will be confessed before the Father—totally accepted in the presence of God.

3:7-13

The church of Philadelphia, which means "brotherly love," was like Smyrna, in that it received no rebukes from Jesus—only applause. This congregation seemed to have an open-door policy, wide open to the Spirit of God. They were small but mighty. They were radically different from Sardis. Sardis had a reputation for being alive but was dead. Philadelphia was very alive. One dead church and one live one.

LASER SURGERY

1. SIGNS OF LIFE

Divide students into groups of three to five. Distribute writing utensils and copies of the student sheet on page 46 of this book. Make sure each group has at least one Bible. Begin by having students read Revelation 3:1-13.

On their sheet, they are to list signs of life and signs of death in the church. For instance, under "signs of life" from Sardis (S) they might list *staying clean before God* and from Philadelphia (P) *keeping God's word* and *not denying his name*. Under "signs of death" from Sardis (S) they might list *deeds were not complete* and from Philadelphia (P) *fading strength*. Share pertinent background information about these two churches from the **Looking Deeper** section.

After students have finished working through the questions in their small groups, ask them:

- **Are we ever guilty of simply going through the motions in our Christian lives—appearing alive, but really being dead spiritually? In what ways do we do that?**
- **How are we like the Pharisees who looked good on the outside but inside were "full of dead men's bones"?**

2. A YOUTH GROUP PHYSICAL

Before class, you will need to draw a horizontal line on the top of a transparency or on a markerboard. On the left side of the line write the phrase, "Hardly ever!" and on the right side of the line the phrase, "All the time!" Underneath the line, write the following statements and Scripture references:

Media Media Media Media Media Media Media

Moment

Show a clip from the movie *Simon Birch*. The smallest kid in town is Simon, but deep down inside he knows that he was born to do something big. Start the clip at 1:34:41 and stop at 1:38:30. Simon helps save some kids from a bus that has slid into a lake.

Then, the clip that begins at 1:42:00 and ends at 1:45:25 shows Simon in bed, dying, but receiving praise from his best friend. Even though he was small, God's purpose in Simon's life was huge. The church at Philadelphia was a small congregation, but the believers had a big mission from God. Ask students:

- **How have we let size discourage us?**
- **Have we ever minimized our abilities and thought "we have little to offer"?**
- **What are some other examples of a small vessel being used to accomplish a mighty task?**

Materials needed:
Reproducible student sheet on page 46 of this book; Bibles; writing utensils

Materials needed:
Marker and markerboard or transparency and overhead projector; Bibles

Materials needed:
Reproducible student sheets on pages 47, 48 of this book; appropriate props and costumes

- **We're seeing students come to Christ (Acts 2:47).**
- **As a group we are serving others (Acts 2:44, 45).**
- **We act the same at school and church (Matthew 23:28).**
- **We show evidence of hunger for God (Matthew 5:6).**
- **We experience persecution at times (1 Peter 4:12-17).**

Begin this activity by asking, **"Has anyone ever had to go to a doctor and get a physical in order to participate in sports at your school? When you take a physical, a doctor checks you over to make sure all your vital signs like your heart rate and blood pressure are normal before he can declare you fit to play a sport. In the same way, we can look at certain tests to evaluate our group's spiritual fitness. Let's check out some of these ways in which we can determine the spiritual health of our group."**

Go down the list one by one, reading each statement and Scripture reference. After each statement, ask students to place on the line an "H" (for health) to indicate how their group is doing in that area. On several of the statements, allow time for students to disagree, moving the "H" back and forth as they determine as a group where it should be placed.

Conclude by asking students:

- **As you review the above, what would you say are our group's strengths?**
- **What are our weaknesses?**

GETTING FOCUSED

1. INSTANT MESSAGE

Ahead of time, you will want to recruit three actors who are good readers. You'll need two girls and one guy. Before class, give them copies of the skit on pages 47, 48 of this book and ask them to become familiar with the sketch. Many of the characters' spoken lines are actually being read off the computer screen before them because they are reading what the other characters have typed in instant messages. The portions of the script that are being read aloud are found in caps. It is the actor's job to distinguish between his or her own lines and the lines being read from the screen in order to not confuse the audience.

Ask your actors to come forward with their laptop computers and present the skit for the other students. Introduce the skit to your group by saying something like this: **"This skit is similar to the movie _You've Got Mail_. Two people are typing instant messages to one another. Let's watch and see what happens."**

After students have presented the skit, applaud their efforts and ask your group:

- **What would it have been like if computers had been in existence when Jesus spoke to the seven churches of Asia?**
- **What if Jesus sent his words of affirmation and rebuke for us today via instant messaging?**

- **Would we sit in silence, feeling guilty or would we try to defend ourselves?**
- **What would we do differently as a result of his words?**

Conclude by asking God to bless your students' efforts to wake up spiritually and live for him.

2. YOUR EPITAPH

Collect several obituary sections of your local newspaper during the week prior to this lesson. To conclude today's study, distribute the obituaries among students. Ask them to read about the deceased and identify some of the positive contributions they made to society.

Ask students:

- **What characteristics made these people likable by those who knew them?**
- **What legacies did they leave behind?**

Record student responses on the board. Then ask:

- **What kinds of things would you like to be remembered for when you die?**
- **What are some positive characteristics of the spiritual lives of others in this room?**

Record these responses as well. Conclude by asking God to bless your students' efforts to wake up spiritually and live for him.

Materials needed:
Obituaries; chalk and chalkboard or marker and markerboard

Media Moment

A great way to close this session would be by playing the song "Speechless," recorded by Steven Curtis Chapman on his *Speechless* album.

Signs
of
Life

Read Revelation 3:1–13.

What are some of the signs of life and signs of death in a church? Below, write in the appropriate column any descriptions Jesus gives to indicate signs of life or death in a church. Write an "S" next to the description if the church referred to is Sardis and a "P" if the church referred to is Philadelphia.

Vital Signs (Alive)	Flat Lines (Dead)
_____	_____
_____	_____
_____	_____
_____	_____
_____	_____

What problem did Jesus have with the Pharisees in Matthew 23:27?

One sign of a living church is persecution. Both Sardis and Philadelphia engaged in prayer, worship and good deeds. Philadelphia experienced persecution while Sardis did not. Why?

46   Lesson 5

Instant Message

Characters: *2 female, 1 male*

This skit is similar to the movie *You've Got Mail*. Many of the characters' spoken lines are actually being read off the computer screen before them because they are reading what the other characters have typed in instant messages. The portions of the script that are being read aloud are found in caps. It is the actor's job to distinguish between his or her own lines and the lines being read from the screen in order to not confuse the audience.

As the scene opens, Lou is seen typing furiously at stage right. He is programming at his computer terminal. He is the typical nerd with suspenders, flood pants, broken glasses and . . . well, you know the type. Frieda, a beautiful girl, is sitting quietly at stage left. She has typed an instant message to Lou and is waiting for a response.

(Lou's computer suddenly speaks in a luscious female voice.)

COMPUTER: *(Beep)* You have an instant message.

LOU: *(Screams in surprise. He believes he has taught his machine to speak.)* Hello! Oh, this is awesome. This is totally neato. OK. Computer, identify my voice. *(Silence)* Computer, identify my voice. *(Silence. Then Lou speaks very loudly.)* Computer, I demand that you identify my voice!

(Lou's sister, Darlene, enters the room.)

DARLENE: What are you doing?

LOU: Darlene, go get Mom. Get Dad. Get everyone . . . bring the dog! I am king of all that I survey!

DARLENE: What are you talking about??

LOU: Apparently, as I was programming simulated neural transmitters into my hard drive, I stumbled upon a second dimensional thought anthrax that I didn't even know existed. I have taught my computer to speak! I am a genius, and you may now kiss my feet.

DARLENE: Hold that thought, oh great one. What exactly did your computer say to you?

LOU: She said, *(Imitating the computer's tone)* "You have an instant message."

DARLENE: *(Goes to look at his computer screen, and then laughs.)* You freak. You have mail.

LOU: Get out of my way, Darlene. I have to program a decoding syntax that will allow me to understand what this means.

DARLENE: Lou, someone has sent you an instant message. A letter. Mail . . . you know? Your computer is just letting you know so that you can read it now.

LOU: Really? No one has ever written to me before. *(He is enthralled.)*

DARLENE: *(Exiting the room)* That's amazing, considering the genius you are.

LOU: *(Opens his e-mail and reads. . .)* HELLO OUT THERE. HOPE YOU DON'T MIND MY WRITING, BUT I'M TOTALLY BORED RIGHT NOW. A/S CHECK??

What's an A/S check? Audio . . . synoptic? Well, here goes . . . *(He begins to type.)*

FRIEDA: *(Her computer beeps and she begins to read . . .)* HI. IN RESPONSE TO THE A/S CHECK . . . I HAVEN'T HAD MUCH TIME TO DELVE INTO THE AUDIO CAPABILITIES OF THIS NEW HARD DRIVE YET, BUT I UNDERSTAND THAT ITS 550 MEGAHERTZ, PLUS THE EXPANDED CACHE SIZE, WILL GIVE ME UNLIMITED OPTIONS. I'M CURRENTLY REROUTING ALL OF MY MEMORY TO BYPASS THE LAME INHERENT PROGRAMMING BIAS OF IBM. AND AS YOU KNOW, MAC COMPUTERS ARE EQUALLY BIASED IN THEIR SEQUENCING.
(To herself) What in the world? *(She types.)*

LOU: *(His computer beeps and he reads . . .)* WHAT DOES ANY OF THAT HAVE TO DO WITH AN AGE/SEX CHECK? Oh! *(He is embarrassed and looks around to be sure no one is looking. He types . . .)*

FRIEDA: *(Beep. She reads . . .)* SORRY. I'M A BOY. *(She rolls her eyes and types . . .)*

LOU: *(Beep. He reads . . .)* DUH. BUT OBVIOUSLY A VERY SMART BOY WHO WILL BE RICH ONE DAY. I LIKE THAT. *(Lou giggles shyly.)* HOW OLD ARE YOU? *(Suddenly he is frightened. He yells for his sister.)* Darlene! Help!

DARLENE: *(Entering his room with her magazine . . .)* What now, Einstein?

LOU: *(Points in fright to his screen.)* It's a girl!

DARLENE: No kidding? A girl is writing my little brother? This I've got to see. *(She reads the interaction so far.)* Good grief, you do need help, little one. OK. You don't want to tell her you're only 14. She's probably a lot older than that, and even if she isn't you'll want her to think you're older. Tell her you're 17.

LOU: I can't do that! It's lying!

DARLENE: Lou, do you want my help or not?

LOU: Not if I have to lie. *(Darlene plops down with her magazine. Lou types . . .)*

FRIEDA: *(Beep. She reads . . .)* I'M 14 YEARS OLD. Hmmmm. OK *(She types . . .)*

LOU: *(Beep. He reads . . .)* TELL ME ABOUT YOU. WHAT DO YOU LOOK LIKE? WHAT ARE YOUR HOBBIES? YOUR FAVE BAND? MOVIE? *(Darlene is engrossed in her magazine and not paying attention. Lou types . . .)*

FRIEDA: *(Beep. She reads . . .)* WELL, I'M ABOUT 5'5", MY EYES ARE BROWN LIKE MY 12-YEAR MOLAR, I WEAR SIZE SMALL IN MEN'S CLOTHING, AND LOVE MATH AND SCIENCE. I LIKE TO LISTEN TO UNDERWATER RECORDINGS OF WHALE SONGS AND STUFF, AND I GUESS MY FAVORITE MOVIE IS "ALGORITHMS IN ACTION," A NEW MATH APPROACH.

LOU: This is fun!

DARLENE: What did you write? *(She looks over his shoulder.)* Lou, you idiot. What are you thinking? Write J/K. Quick! J/K!

LOU: What? JFK?

DARLENE: *(Shoving him from his chair.)* Move . . . quick! Man, if you ever get married I'm going to keel over. *(She types . . .)*

FRIEDA: *(Beeps. She is relieved to see the J/K and she types . . .)*

DARLENE: *(Beeps. She reads . . .)* I THOUGHT YOU WERE J/K! NO ONE COULD BE THAT LAME. *(Suddenly, she becomes defensive of her brother. She angrily types . . .)*

FRIEDA: *(Beeps. She reads . . .)* WHO ARE YOU CALLING LAME? MY BROTHER IS NOT LAME. HE'S SMARTER IN JUST HIS LITTLE TOE THAN YOU AND I ARE COMBINED. *(Looking confused, Frieda types . . . .)*

DARLENE: *(Beeps. She reads . . .)* BROTHER? I'M SO CONFUSED. A/S CHECK? *(She types . . .)*

LOU: Darlene, let me talk to her. Come on. Darlene . . . get up. Move! *(Darlene keeps typing.)*

FRIEDA: *(Beeps. She reads . . .)* FEMALE. SIXTEEN. I'M LOU'S SISTER, BUT I'D PREFER TO BE THE ONLY ONE CALLING HIM LAME, WHICH HE ONLY SOMETIMES IS. *(She smiles, relaxing, and types . . .)*

DARLENE: *(Beeps. She reads . . .)* COOL. MY BAD. I'M SIXTEEN, TOO. WHERE DO YOU LIVE? *(Darlene is busy writing her new friend . . .)*

LOU: *(Disgustedly, as he leaves his own room.)* I liked it better when I didn't have mail.

YOU MAKE ME SICK!

Hot or cold; "on fire" or part of the "frozen chosen." Your students have probably witnessed some believers they would classify as either one or the other. Then, they know a whole host of others who are neither hot nor cold, choosing instead to ride the fence—trying to get the best of both worlds. These people act one way in one situation and just the opposite in another. Jesus says these things ought not to be. In fact, it is such a despicable situation that it makes him sick. Pray that as you prepare to teach this session, God will pull the blinders off your students' eyes and help them see where they have allowed themselves to settle for mediocrity.

EYE-POPPING OPENERS

1. SPIRITUAL BLINDNESS

After all of your students have arrived, choose one person to be "It." Ask another adult to escort the student out of the classroom until you are ready for him to return. While "It" is out of the room, instruct the group to sit in chairs in a circle, and choose another student to be the "leader voice." This is the voice that "It" needs to listen to very carefully. Also, instruct the group that everyone else must shout opposite instructions from those of the leader voice when the activity begins, making it virtually impossible for "It" to hear the leader voice.

Have your volunteer return. Explain that the leader voice will be a certain person and "It" must listen carefully and follow only the instructions of the leader voice concerning where to go, no matter what everyone else is saying.

Blindfold your volunteer. At this point, everyone else should swap seats, including the leader voice. Spin the blindfolded student around a few times. Have everyone begin yelling directions at him. (Ask the leader voice to use a somewhat softer, steady, but determined tone.) The leader voice should attempt to guide him to the leader.

Remove the blindfold, then ask the student:

• **Was it easy or hard to hear the leader voice? Why?**

Conclude this activity by saying, **"There are so many voices in our culture today begging for our attention. If we are spiritually blind, we will neither see nor hear God. In order to clearly hear**

LESSON TEXT
Revelation 3:14-22

LESSON FOCUS
The believers in the seventh and last church, Laodicea, are indicted for being lukewarm in their faith.

LESSON GOALS
As a result of participating in this lesson, students will:
• Grasp what contributes to a lukewarm spirit.
• Recognize why Jesus dislikes halfhearted devotion.
• Explore solutions to their spiritual blindness.
• Evaluate their preparedness for Christ's return.

Materials needed:
Blindfold

his voice, we need to pull off the blindfold and listen closely. Such was the case of the last church in Revelation for whom Jesus had an important message. Let's check it out."

2. JUST LIMERICK IT!

Begin by reading Revelation 3:14-22 from a modern paraphrase such as THE MESSAGE. Distribute writing utensils and blank paper to each student.

Comment, **"We are going to begin today by letting you exercise your creative gifts. You are going to write a limerick based on these verses. A limerick has a poem-like symmetry to it. The first, second and fifth lines rhyme, as do the third and fourth lines. Here is an example:**

'There were those neither hot nor cold
Who lived their lives out so bold
They were unaware of what they lacked
Then they were God's yack
And left on the ground to mold.'
Now, it's your turn."

Give students five to eight minutes to craft their limericks. Then have some share with the rest of the group. Conclude this activity by saying, **"As we finish up our study on the seven churches of Revelation, today we're going to discover some believers who received some pretty strong words from Jesus—and the message they received wasn't just a nice little poem."**

Materials needed:
Paper; writing utensils; Bible

Media Moment

Play the song "Brighten My Heart," recorded by Sixpence None the Richer on the Rocketown Records *Exodus* compilation project.

Media Moment

Show several short clips from the movie *October Sky*, which is based on a true story. In 1957 nobody gave Homer Hickham, Jr. a chance to win the rocket science contest, especially from tiny Coalwood, West Virginia. Against all odds, Homer won the contest! His passion and persistence paid off. The clips are as follows: Start at counter 1:18:25 and end at 1:19:40 (Homer tells his dad he wants to go into space, rather than work in the coal mine. The scene ends with his father walking away.); 1:29:33 to 1:30:59 (the awards ceremony); 1:32:52 to 1:34:37 (Homer talks to his dad about his dream to fly).

After showing the clips, ask students:

- **What obstacles, like Homer, do you face in order to follow your dreams?**
- **What are some of the ways we allow our hearts to become lukewarm toward Christ, rather than continuing to pursue our passion for him?**

LOOKING DEEPER

REVELATION 3:14-16

The church of Laodicea is given one big rebuke for being spiritually lukewarm. They were neither hot nor cold. Laodicea was the wealthiest city of all seven of the cities we have studied, but spiritually they were very poor. Why did Jesus say this church made him sick?

Although Laodicea was known for its materialism, banking industry and incredible medical school, the city had a water problem. The *Life Application Bible* summarizes the problem: "At one time an aqueduct was built to bring water to the city from hot springs. But by the time the water reached the city, it was neither hot nor refreshingly cool—only lukewarm. The church had become as bland as the tepid water that came into the city."[1]

THE MESSAGE uses some striking language when it paraphrases verses 15-17: "I know you inside and out, and find little to my liking. You're not cold, you're not hot—far better to be either cold or hot! You're stale. You're stagnant. You make me want to vomit. You brag, 'I'm rich, I've got it made, I need nothing from anyone,' oblivious that in fact you're a pitiful, blind beggar, threadbare and homeless."

3:17-22

Contrary to popular opinion, materialism is not a sign of spiritual blessing. In fact, just the opposite. James 1:9, 10 points out that many people who suffer financially are rich in faith. The Laodiceans had become spiritually blind. Materialism has a way of doing that to people. The key to life? Repent and open the door to a relationship with Jesus.

"Up on your feet, then! About face! Run after God! Look at me. I stand at the door. I knock. If you hear me call and open the door, I'll come right in and sit down to supper with you" (vv. 19, 20, THE MESSAGE). Jesus wants us to be on fire for him. Instead of living apathetic, mediocre lives, he desires that we be ready for his coming. Then, we'll be able to sit down with him at the dinner table for the most incredible feast we could ever imagine.

LASER SURGERY

1. HOT OR COLD?

Begin this activity by inviting several students to share a time when they ate something that made them sick to their stomach. After several students have shared their gross-out stories, ask them to gather in groups of three to five people. Distribute writing utensils and copies of the student sheet on page 54 of this book. Make sure each group has at least one Bible. If you didn't read it at the beginning of the session, ask students to read Revelation 3:14-22.

Give groups plenty of time to answer the questions on the student sheet. After they have completed their work, brainstorm with them concerning this question: **"What are some ways we can be 'hot' for God in these arenas?"** On the board, write across the top the three phrases: **at school**, **at home** and **with friends.** Ask students to respond to your question in each of these areas. As they share, write their reactions under the appropriate column.

Conclude this activity by saying, **"Just as it was no fun when you ate something that made you sick, it's no picnic for our Lord when we upset his stomach. Let's see what he would have us do about it."**

2. TASTE TEST

Bring in a variety of drinks, such as iced tea, hot chocolate, a cola, root beer, cold coffee and lukewarm yogurt. Ask for a volunteer and blindfold him without letting him see the drinks you have. Choose one of your drinks, pour it in a cup and see if he can identify what it is. Choose different students for each of your drinks, each time asking the person to describe a particular taste.

After removing the blindfold, some questions you might ask each volunteer include these:

- **Have you ever been really sick with a fever, chills or vomiting? Give us some details.**

Media Moment

Show several clips from the video *The Truman Show*. Truman Burbank is the "live" star of the Truman Show, which is broadcast 24 hours a day. For years, millions have watched Truman's real life unfold on TV, unbeknownst to him. But slowly, and progressively, Truman sees the light. He is ready to change, to break free (similar to the biblical meaning of the word "repent").

The clip that begins at 1:24:56 and ends at 1:33:40 shows Truman ready to start over again. Then, beginning at 1:34:21 and ending at 1:35:48, Truman breaks free from "The Truman Show."

The church of Laodicea was in a rut and needed to break free, to change, to repent of their lukewarmness.

Materials needed:
Reproducible sheet on page 54 of this book; Bibles; writing utensils; chalk and chalkboard or marker and markerboard

Media Moment

Show the skit entitled "The Lukewarm Gang" from the *Shock Wave, Vol. 1* video. This segment imagines what it might be like if people actually threw up whenever they acted hypocritical in their Christian lives. This video can be ordered by calling (213) 413-0676 or visit Ground Zero Productions at gzero@earthlink.net.

Materials needed:
Various drinks; plastic cups; blindfold; Bibles

Materials needed:
Thermostat; thermometer

- **What do you like about a hot drink? A cold drink?**
- **What do you dislike about a hot drink? A cold drink?**
- **Have you ever had a lukewarm food or drink? How did it affect you?**

If you haven't already done so, read Revelation 3:14-22. Then ask students, **"Why do you think Jesus referred to this church as lukewarm?"** Refer to the background information in the **Looking Deeper** section for help.

GETTING FOCUSED

1. THERMOSTAT OR THERMOMETER?

Bring to your classroom a thermometer and a thermostat. As you share the following illustration, refer to the objects in your hands.

"Do you know the difference between a thermostat and a thermometer? A thermometer merely tells what the temperature is in a particular place. If your thermometer reads sixty degrees and you place that thermometer in a room that is currently seventy degrees, the thermometer will change to register whatever the room temperature is. It won't be long before the thermometer reads seventy degrees. It always adjusts to its environment.

"On the other hand, a thermostat actually adjusts the temperature of a specific room. If the thermostat is set at sixty degrees and the room is seventy degrees, the temperature of the room will eventually conform to the thermostat's setting. The room will become sixty degrees."

Ask students:

- **What do you want to be, a thermometer or a thermostat? We can change the environment around us or let the environment change us. Jesus calls us to be thermostats.**
- **What keeps people from changing?**
- **What prevents people from breaking free from destructive habits?**

Conclude by providing students with some private solitude in which they evaluate their relationship with God. Read aloud Revelation 3:20 from THE MESSAGE: **"Look at me. I stand at the door. I knock. If you hear me call and open the door, I'll come right in and sit down to supper with you."**

Ask students to quietly think about this question: **"Is Jesus knocking on certain parts of your life to become alive to him? Pray that he will be so excited about your temperature for him, that he will want to come and feast with you."**

2. WHICH ARE WE?

This activity provides a great summary of what your students have learned about each of the seven churches in this study. Allow students to gather in groups of three to five people. Distribute writing utensils and copies of the student sheet on page 55 of this book. Have Bibles available for students' reference.

Depending on the size of your group, assign each group of students one or two churches. They will read the Scripture that pertains to their church, then identify Jesus' words of encouragement and his words of correction to that particular body of believers.

After each group has completed its work, bring all the groups back together and ask students:

- **Which of these seven churches is most like our group? Why?** (Allow students to discuss and defend their varied responses.)
- **Which of these seven churches is most like your individual life?**

Don't ask for students to respond publicly, but rather to think silently about their answers. Close by encouraging them to pray about those things in their lives for which Jesus would have words of correction.

Materials needed:
Reproducible sheet on page 55 of this book; Bibles; writing utensils

Check This . . .

Create a continuum of spiritual temperatures, with a one being cold and a ten signifying hot. Ask one student to hold up a card with "one" written on it and another with "ten" written on it. Have the two students stand apart fifteen feet or more, asking your group to silently identify where they are spiritually. Encourage them to stand where they think they *really* are. Point out that if they are standing at a point anywhere less than a seven, they are probably "lukewarm."

Check This . . .

Have students create role plays that portray each of these scenarios:
- Someone who is "cold" about God— "couldn't care less" attitude
- Someone who is "hot" for God—"on fire" for him
- Someone who is "lukewarm"— apathetic toward spiritual things

Hot or Cold?

What contemporary phrases come to mind when you hear the following words?

Hot (example: *passionate*)

Cold

Lukewarm

What do people mean when they say "He is on fire for God"?

What are some ways that we can tell someone is "hot" for God?

Mark 12:30, 31

John 14:15

Romans 12:1, 2

What are some ways that people show they are "cold" for God?

Compare James 2:14-17 with Revelation 3:15, 16. What do we learn here about deeds performed for God?

What reaction does Jesus have to those who are lukewarm in their response to him? (Revelation 3:16)

What does it mean to be spiritually lukewarm?

What advice does Jesus give in Revelation 3:19, 20 for overcoming spiritual lukewarmness?

WHICH ARE WE?

Ephesus   Pergamum
Thyatira   Philadelphia
Smyrna   Laodicea

Ephesus (Revelation 2:1-7)

Words of encouragement

Words of correction

Smyrna (Revelation 2:8-11)

Words of encouragement

Words of correction

Pergamum (Revelation 2:12-17)

Words of encouragement

Words of correction

Thyatira (Revelation 2:18-29)

Words of encouragement

Words of correction

Sardis (Revelation 3:1-6)

Words of encouragement

Words of correction

Philadelphia (Revelation 3:7-13)

Words of encouragement

Words of correction

Laodicea (Revelation 3:14-22)

Words of encouragement

Words of correction

Our Youth Group

Words of encouragement

Words of correction

THE UNDERGROUND CHURCH

Where to play: Your choice, indoor, outdoor or both. This game can be played by anywhere from ten to 500 students and usually works better at night.

Time limit: 20 minutes to an hour and a half

Purpose of the game: To teach students to stand up for their faith and let them catch a glimpse of what it might be like for a persecuted church in the end times. Eventually, there will be a "rapture" into the presence of Jesus.

RULES OF THE GAME: PART 1

There are two teams, one trying to find the hidden underground church, and the other trying to prevent them from finding it. Designate one team "Secret Police" and the other "Christians." There should be more Christians than Secret Police. Designate two places, a jail and a secret underground church. The Christians' goal is to make it safely to the underground church. The Secret Police try to keep the Christians from making it to the church by capturing them and throwing them into jail. A Christian is caught by getting tagged. Once a Christian is caught, he must go to jail and cannot escape.

No one knows where the underground church is, not even the Secret Police. Before the game begins, all of the police are given pieces of paper. One of the pieces of paper has the location of the church written on it. The policeman who receives this piece of paper automatically becomes the "Undercover Christian." His or her job is to tell the Christians where the church is located. This must remain a secret, because if the undercover Christian is discovered, then the rest of the Secret Police can throw him in jail also. (If you have a larger group, you might want to designate more than one undercover Christian.)

Once a Christian is tagged, the Secret Police asks him if he is a Christian. If the person says yes, then the Secret Police can take him to jail. If the person denies his or her faith and says no, then the person is free to go. The Christians should not be told ahead of time about this question. Let them make the decision concerning what they will say.

After a Christian discovers the underground church, he is safe while he is there, but the believer has the option of going out and telling other Christians the location of the church. This is done at his own risk—once he leaves the safety of the church he can get caught and be taken back to jail!

TEXT
Revelation 4:1-11

FOCUS
The scene is in Heaven, where the saints of God are worshiping the Lamb. But first, we will simulate an underground church experience for believers.

GOALS
As a result of participating in this event, students will:
- Imagine what Heaven might be like in the eternal presence of God.
- Discover the power of unity in the midst of persecution.
- Participate in an authentic, interactive worship experience.

Check This . . .

- When the rules for the underground church are given, it is important to tell students that those who choose the only true church will be rewarded at the end of the game. Do not tell them that they will be rewarded with a crown.
- Make sure you lock all necessary doors; you don't want students going into and unlocking doors that are not okay for them to enter.
- Notify those who need to be aware of your activities (church officials, fire department, police department, neighbors).

OPTIONAL IDEAS STUDENTS WON'T FORGET!

(Yes, these have all been done!)

• Choose your Secret Police ahead of time (possibly using volunteer youth workers). Have them dress in camouflage, wear face paint and carry flashlights. People who are in the military usually have more than one set of fatigues if you need to borrow them. (Or, you could simply use red armbands to identify the Secret Police.)

• Use an air-raid siren, to broadcast the beginning of the experience, signifying that chaos has begun. Keep the air-raid siren and other sound effects going till the end of the game. Most music stores have CDs that have sound effects on them, such as war sounds.

• Just before you start the siren, show a skit about someone dying for his faith, and use the air-raid siren to signal the end of the drama and the beginning of the game.

• Shut down all of the lights on your campus.

• Put manned spotlights on the roofs of your buildings giving a wartime or prison feel to the campus. You can rent these for about $40 from places that do big events.

• Place speakers in buildings, pointing outside of windows. Play sound effects such as helicopters, machine-gun fire of planes going overhead or other war sounds. This gives a great effect.

• Ask the military to bring some of their vehicles out and leave them sitting around or even drive them around the campus. (Yes, we have done this!)

• Use fog machines and red lights close to windows of buildings to give the appearance of an "on-fire effect."

• Place strobe lights in trees to give some lighting effects.

• Use large smoke bombs around the campus.

• Have someone with a microphone broadcast over a sound system a warning for Christians to give up—that the Secret Police and the government are there only to "help them."

• Have Secret Police rappel down the sides of some buildings.

• Hang menacing flags off the sides of buildings to make it feel like you are in another country or time period.

• Have each Christian carry an ID card; whenever a Secret Police catches a Christian, he asks to see his ID card. The Secret Police asks if the person is a Christian. If he denies it, the police writes down his ID# and lets him go. At the end of the game, the students are asked to look at the numbers on their cards as the numbers are read. This helps make an impact about denying one's faith. Laminate the ID cards to make a cool souvenir of the game.

• Use 50-gallon metal drums with holes cut in the bottom of them. Put firewood in them to burn for effect and for light. Post a guard who does not want to run around a lot at each of the drums and make sure he has a fire extinguisher. These are good if you turn the lights off and you need lights around stairs and other hazardous places.

• Instead of using a jail, call it an "institution" where Christians can go and get help for their "faulty thinking."

• In the institution, have different rooms where different levels of interrogation take place, each one threatening Christians to either deny God by taking the mark (a hand stamp) or to face death for their faith.

• At the final stage of the interrogation, have a room where you have a Christian guard planted who has a recording of gunfire. The Christian guard will save the lives of the Christians but they have to scream when the recording of the gunfire is played. That way, the others being interrogated will think that death awaits them if they don't take the mark. Those Christians are then freed to go back out and try to find the church. It's a good idea to interrogate the Christians in groups so they won't get too scared—especially if some of them are visiting your group for the first time!

• Have a meeting place somewhere on campus where Secret Police will take their prisoners to get into a van. Take the seats out of the van and cover the windows so the Christians cannot see out. Have a guard in the back making sure everyone is intimidated and keeping everyone quiet. Drive the van around so it seems like you are going somewhere and then drop them off at the institution to "get treatment." Then go back and get more Christians.

• Have a pastor, worship leader or worship band at the underground church so students know they have found it.

• Have more than one church. One is the true church and one or more are not "true churches." That will force students to listen to the message and ask questions to the pastors who are preaching. Don't tell students there are any more churches—just tell them to be careful what they hear. This helps students to think about how in the end times there are going to be lots of groups claiming to be the true church.

One way to do this is by having false pastors and prophets make the students do stupid religious things like stand on their heads or lie on the ground. Dress one of the false prophets up like Jesus. Students will get the point that there are some weird things out there. (If you do this, you'll need to debrief it at the end, explaining that there were false churches. Identify the different pastors so the students don't leave thinking that they were at the true church if they were not.)

• Have the true church move locations every 20 minutes or so. The Christians may have to be on the move so that they won't get caught. This gets interesting when a Christian leaves the safety of the underground church to go rescue his fellow believers, whom he can no longer find.

• Have civilians dressed up in wigs and coats, who serve as informants. They mill around and give information to the Christians about the underground church.

RULES OF THE GAME: PART 2

The underground church concludes with a "rapture" experience. It may be as formal or informal as you wish. You may choose to obtain a variety of decorations for a "heavenly" atmosphere or you may decide to keep it informal with a strict focus on worship. Consider the following suggestions:

You will likely have a time set aside to end the underground church. As the jail fills and false churches are busy deceiving naive believers, Jesus and his angels are preparing to "come to earth." They should be dressed and ready with their supplies at least thirty minutes before the end of the underground church. Jesus, the angels and the instrumentalists begin their "processional" at fifteen minutes before the game ends. As they walk from their prep location, the instrumentalists play worship songs consistent with the rapture. (It is not suggested that anyone sing at this time.) Those who see Jesus as he is walking must not speak to him unless he speaks to them. The processional appears with Jesus in front, instrumentalists behind him and finally the angels with flaming torches. When the processional reaches its first location, the transition is complete.

RAPTURE

The first stop Jesus makes will be in the jail. It is important the audience *hear* music before they see the processional. As Jesus appears to the prisoners, his angels should surround them on all sides. Jesus explains that he has come to free them and bring them home. He then instructs everyone to follow him. As the prisoners join in the processional, the rapture is under way.

The second stop is the underground church. Jesus appears to them in the same way he appeared to the prisoners. First, music is heard, then Jesus appears and greets everyone while the angels surround them. The prisoners greet the church as well. Jesus explains he has come to free all believers and bring them home to Heaven. From here, everyone follows Jesus to a previously chosen worship location. During the processional, music is played continuously and the "raptured" believers may begin singing. The angels continue to carry their flaming torches.

Ideally, the false churches will be positioned so the processional from the underground church to the worship location will pass by them. In this scenario, the false churches fall behind the processional and meet at the worship location.

WORSHIP

All "believers" and "unbelievers" have assembled together in one location. As the believers (those who were in the underground church or jail) are entering the worship area, they are given a crown which they are instructed to wear. Believers and unbelievers are also given small copies of music and Scripture verses. While everyone is arriving for worship, Jesus stands before them and quotes Revelation 4:1: **"Come**

Check This . . .

You will need the following for your transition time and rapture:
- Five white robes (Jesus and angels)
- Sandals
- Individuals who play instruments (such as trumpets, drums, guitars, etc.)
- Torches (optional—if used, the angels chosen should be adults rather than students)

Check This . . .

The following items are needed for this time of worship:
- A worship location (indoor or outdoor)
- Handmade crowns
- Instrumentalists
- Candles and wax drip protectors
- Copies of worship songs
- Copies of verses from Revelation 4 (Hand-size sheets for music and Scripture verses work best because candles are being used)

up here, and I will show you what must take place after these things" (NASB). At this time the angels and instrumentalists begin singing "Holy, Holy, Holy," instructing the audience to join them. Jesus turns his back to the audience and lifts his hands toward Heaven. As they are singing, the believers are instructed to bring their crowns and place them at Jesus' feet. In return for his or her crown, each believer receives a lighted and unlighted candle with wax drip protector. Each "believer" offers his lit candle to an "unbeliever" and lights it for him.

Continue with the worship songs from the music sheets. You may wish to have a list of songs chosen beforehand or allow the students to call out their choices. At this time you may also wish to have the individual playing the role of Jesus leave the scene. From here on, the individual prompt is not needed as the students are offering true worship to Jesus Christ.

Encourage students to offer praises to God from the Scripture verse sheets. For example, they can repeat Revelation 4:11: **"You are worthy, our Lord and God, to receive glory and honor and power, for you created all things, and by your will they were created and have their being."** Offer verses quoted in unison. Offer prayers of worship, encouraging students to pray aloud. Continue with songs, prayers and Scriptures as you feel the Spirit leading your group. When you are nearing your conclusion, dispose of the candles and encourage everyone to join hands.

CONCLUSION

With joined hands, announce together in a loud voice: **"Worthy is the Lamb, who was slain, to receive power and wealth and wisdom and strength and honor and glory and praise! . . . To him who sits on the throne and to the Lamb be praise and honor and glory and power, for ever and ever!"** (Revelation 5:12, 13).

Conclude the event by saying something like this: **"We are really excited you came. We trust that you know Jesus personally and received a little taste of what is to come. If you need to talk with someone concerning how to become a Christian, there are people here who can help you. Thanks for coming. May the Lord go with you."** Play some praise music as people leave or stick around to visit with each other.

Check This . . .

Suggested Scripture verses include the following:
- Revelation 4:8
- Revelation 4:11
- Revelation 5:9, 10
- Revelation 5:12, 13

Media Media Media Media Moment

Some suggested hymns and choruses include these:

"Holy, Holy, Holy," "Thou Art Worthy," "Crown Him With Many Crowns," "All Hail the Power of Jesus' Name," "Amazing Grace," "Joyful, Joyful We Adore Thee," "The Hallelujah Chorus," "King of Kings," "We Bow Down," "Father, I Adore You," "I Love You, Lord," "Lord, I Lift Your Name on High," "Victory Chant," "Jesus, Name Above All Names," "We Will Glorify," "Open the Eyes of My Heart," "Be Glorified," "Agnus Dei," "Your Love Oh Lord" and "Salvation Belongs to Our God."

Contributors

Craig Garrison has been in youth ministry for ten years. Craig made contributions to lessons two and four. Craig and his wife Kara have three daughters and a son.

John Kesel served as a youth pastor for almost ten years and recently completed a Master of Divinity degree at Asbury Theological Seminary. He contributed to lessons three and six. John is married to Debby.

Mark and Amy Whaley are a husband-wife youth pastor team in Orlando, Florida. They provided many additional ideas for the bonus event.

Jonathan and Suzie Weibel serve in the youth ministry at the Christian and Missionary Alliance Church in State College, Pennsylvania. They contributed to lesson five and provided a number of sketches and crowdbreakers throughout the book.

NOTES

LESSON 1

[1]Charles Swindoll, *Letters to Churches* study guide (Anaheim, CA: Insight for Living), p. 6.

[2]Max Lucado, *When Christ Comes* (Nashville: Word Publishing, 1999), p. 132.

[3]Eugene Peterson, *Reversed Thunder* (San Francisco: Harper Publishing, 1988), pp. 36, 37.

LESSON 2

[1]Richard Selzer, *Mortal Lessons: Notes on the Art of Surgery*. Copyright © 1974, 1975, 1976, 1987 by Richard Selzer. Reprinted by permission of Georges Borchardt, Inc.

LESSON 3

[1]*Christianity Today*, editorial by Haddon W. Robinson, October 26, 1992. Copyright © 1992 by Christianity Today, Inc. Reprinted by permission.

LESSON 4

[1]*Hot Illustrations for Youth Talks*, copyright © 1994 by Youth Specialties, Inc., 300 South Pierce St., El Cajon, CA 92020. Used by permission.

LESSON 5

[1]John Stott, *What Christ Thinks of the Church* (Wheaton, IL: Harold Shaw Publishers, 1990), p. 79.

LESSON 6

[1]*Life Application Bible* (Wheaton, IL: Tyndale House Publishers, 1991), p. 2306.

Other EMPOWERED® youth products
from Standard Publishing

WHAT'S THE BIG DEAL ABOUT SEX?
order # 23315   (ISBN 0-7847-1099-6)

By Jim Burgen

In a national survey of teens, 99% said their number-one concern is how to say no to sexual pressure. Did you know:
- AIDS has been the sixth leading cause of death among 15–24 year olds since 1991?
- Every day 2,700 teens become pregnant?
- Every 24 hours, another 3,000 lose their virginity?
- Of those that become pregnant, more than three in ten choose to abort the baby?

But God has a better way. The *big deal* is that God has an awesome plan for this generation. In a direct, humorous and compelling way the author gives real answers to questions about waiting, dating, homosexuality, interracial dating, dealing with mistakes and more. And each chapter gives readers an opportunity to get personal with questions for reflection. Whether you work with junior-high or senior-high teens, this award-winning book will help you deal with this hot topic in a relevant way.

WHAT'S THE BIG DEAL ABOUT MY PARENTS?

By Jim Burgen

Veteran youth pastor Jim Burgen has been referred to as "the youth pastor you'd long for your children to know." He has been a road pastor with contemporary Christian bands Audio Adrenaline and the O.C. Supertones. Once again, he takes a mentoring approach to his teenage readers. He offers a straightforward, heart-to-heart, biblical discussion about parental issues with such chapter titles as "The Brady Bunch, the Partridge Family, Joseph and Moses" and "The Trust Factor." Chapters deal with hot topics such as rules, resolving conflicts, communication and living as a Christian in a non-Christian home. And each chapter gives readers an opportunity to get personal with questions for reflection. The *big deal* is that God has a big plan for students and everything that is happening to them right now (for good or bad) he will use to prepare them for the rest of their lives.

order # 23335   (ISBN 0-7847-1252-2)

REBECCA ST. JAMES 40 DAYS WITH GOD (new edition)
a devotional journey

Australian-born Rebecca St. James is a 23-year-old prolific singer/songwriter who has been providing soul-searching lyrics since the age of 16. A modern woman with a strong moral fiber, Rebecca lives what she believes. Her passion is to worship God and serve others in need. Having just released her fifth studio album, *Transform*, Rebecca continues to touch the lives of millions of teenagers worldwide. The strength of this Grammy-award-winning singer is her deep personal walk with God. This best-selling devotional has sold more than 75,000 copies. The new edition of this inspiring, spiral-bound journal features eight pages of full-color scrapbook photos and five bonus devotions. Also included are:
- Journal entries from Rebecca
- Powerful insights from God's Word
- "You Talk to God" journal pages for the reader

order # 23338   (ISBN 0-7847-1274-3)

The Revelation Epic
preparing youth groups for the earth's final days

By David Olshine

Will the world end in a cataclysmic earthquake? Will a great war bring about the final days? And, what do today's high school students need to know? *The Revelation Epic* will help teens get a handle on some of their questions about the future.conclude with.

This book contains six sessions and a bonus event with reproducible student sheets, commentary on the Scripture text and more.

order # 23334   (ISBN 0-7847-1301-4)

STAND YOUR GROUND
a Creative Study of 1st Peter

By Michael Warden

Say no to compromise! This hard-hitting study of 1 Peter challenges students to stop slipping through life with a pseudo-commitment to Christ, one based on convenience rather than conviction.

As they choose to be different from the world students may encounter ridicule, persecution & suffering. For senior-high teens. A bonus session helps students discover some ways in which they can help persecuted Christians worldwide.

order # 23322   (ISBN 0-7847-1152-6)

EMPOWERED® YOUTH PRODUCTS

TO ORDER, CONTACT YOUR LOCAL CHRISTIAN BOOKSTORE.
IF THE BOOK IS OUT OF STOCK, YOU CAN ORDER BY CALLING
or visit www.standardpub.com 1.800.543.1353.

C801